hamlyn cookery club

Chocolate
cookbook

hamlyn cookery club

Chocolate
cookbook

First published in 1999 by Hamlyn
an imprint of Octopus Publishing Group
2–4 Heron Quays
London E14 4JP

British Library Cataloguing-in-Publication Data
A catalogue record for this book is available from the
British Library.

ISBN 0 600 59905 1

Printed in China

Publishing Director: Laura Bamford
Copy Editor: Hilaire Walden
Creative Director: Keith Martin
Design Manager: Bryan Dunn
Designer: Martin Topping
Jacket Photography: Sean Myers
Picture Researchers: Stevie Moe and Christine Junemann
Senior Production Controller: Katherine Hockley

Notes

1 Both metric and imperial measurements have been given in
all recipes. Use one set of measurements only and not a
mixture of both.

2 Standard level spoon measurements are used in all recipes.
1 tablespoon = one 15 ml spoon
1 teaspoon = one 5 ml spoon

3 Eggs should be medium unless otherwise stated.

4 Milk should be full fat unless otherwise stated.

5 Ovens should be preheated to the specified temperature
– if using a fan-assisted oven, follow the manufacturer's
instructions for adjusting the time and temperature.

6 Measurements for canned food have been given as a
standard metric equivalent.

Contents

Introduction

TYPES OF CHOCOLATE

Chocolate comes from cocoa beans, but there is far more to the manufacture of chocolate than grinding cocoa beans. Chocolate is the result of blending different types of beans from a variety of sources that are fermented, dried, roasted, ground and mixed. The bean blend, the precise method, and the amount of cocoa mass and cocoa butter, known collectively as cocoa solids, determine the taste and quality of a chocolate.

Plain Chocolate Plain chocolates contain a minimum of 30% cocoa solids; nearly all chocolate has the cocoa solids content on the wrapper. It is usually recommended that chocolate for cooking should have at least 50% cocoa solids. Nearly all the rest of the contents is sugar, so the lower the cocoa solids content, the sweeter the chocolate.

Milk Chocolate Most milk chocolates contain only about 20% cocoa solids, the legal minimum, so have a milder flavour than plain chocolate, and are sweeter. In the past condensed milk was used, but nowadays dried milk is usually added.

Couverture Chocolate Couverture chocolate is a high quality product that is used by professionals. It has at least 31% cocoa solids, so melts easily and smoothly and sets to a fine gloss.

White Chocolate Some people claim that white chocolate is not really chocolate because it does not contain any cocoa mass, and only some white chocolates contain cocoa butter. It has a very mild, sweet flavour so in cooking it is usually used for making products that contrast with plain chocolate. It does not keep as well as milk and plain chocolates.

Chocolate-flavoured Cake Covering This is an imitation chocolate product that is intended for cooking purposes. It is cheaper than true chocolate but has an inferior flavour, texture and appearance.

STORAGE

Chocolate should be stored in a cool, but not cold, dry, airy place. Wrap opened chocolate in foil or clingfilm and keep away from foods with strong odours.

MELTING CHOCOLATE

Care should be taken when melting chocolate because if it is overheated or it comes into contact with steam, it will 'seize' into a hard mass. Seized chocolate can be rescued by beating in a few drops of flavourless oil or unsalted butter, but if the chocolate is then used for covering or decoration it will not be as glossy.

Saucepan Method Break or grate the chocolate into a heatproof bowl and put the bowl over, not in, a saucepan of hot water. Leave until the chocolate has melted, stirring it occasionally until smooth. If chocolate is melted with milk, cream or butter it can be heated directly over a very low heat, if a heavy-based pan is used. There should be enough liquid to adequately cover the base of the pan. Stir the mixture and take care not to let the chocolate become too hot.

Microwave Method Put no more than 75–125 g (3–4 oz) broken or grated chocolate in a microwave bowl and heat on FULL power. Remove from the microwave and stir until smooth. 75 g (3 oz) chocolate will take 3 minutes.

CHOCOLATE DECORATIONS

Chocolate Curls Use chocolate that is at room temperature, and work over a plate. Draw the blade of a potato peeler along the edge of the bar of chocolate and let the curls fall on to the plate.

Long Curls (Chocolate Scrolls and Chocolate Caraque) Pour melted chocolate on to a marble slab or cool work surface and spread to a thickness of 3 mm (⅛ inch). Leave until cooled and on the point of setting. Put the blade of a long, sharp knife on the chocolate at an angle of 45°. Press the blade firmly against the marble or surface and push slowly away from you to roll the chocolate into a neat cylinder.

Chocolate Leaves Select fresh, glossy leaves that have not been sprayed with pesticides or insecticides, and have distinct veins. Wash and dry the leaves. Melt the chocolate then pull the underside of each leaf along the surface of the chocolate until well coated, or paint chocolate on to the underside of the leaves using a pastry brush or small paint brush. Leave to set. With the tips of your fingers, carefully peel away the leaves. If necessary, veins can be marked on chocolate leaves with a pin or needle.

Desserts

Orange Black Magic Pudding

During baking, the pudding separates into a moist sponge and orange custard.

50 g (2 oz) sunflower margarine
50 g (2 oz) soft brown sugar
50 g (2 oz) caster sugar
grated rind of 1 orange
2 eggs, separated
50 g (2 oz) self-raising flour
15 g (½ oz) cocoa powder
300 ml (½ pint) milk
juice of 1 orange, strained
icing sugar, for dusting

Grease a 1.2 litre (2 pint) ovenproof dish and put in a roasting tin. Beat together the margarine, brown sugar, caster sugar and orange rind in a bowl until light and fluffy. Add the egg yolks and beat well.

Sift the flour and cocoa powder together, then fold into the mixture with the milk and orange juice.

Whisk the egg whites until stiff and fold into the mixture. Spoon into the dish. Half-fill the tin with water. Bake in a preheated oven, 200°C (400°F), Gas Mark 6, for 45–50 minutes until risen and firm. Dust with icing sugar. Serve hot with single cream or natural yogurt.

Serves 4

Apricot and Prune Tart

165 g (5½ oz) plain flour
1 tablespoon cocoa powder
1 tablespoon drinking chocolate powder
40 g (1½ oz) margarine
40 g (1½ oz) lard or white vegetable fat
1½ tablespoons water
grated chocolate, to decorate
Filling:
75 g (3 oz) prunes, soaked overnight
75 g (3 oz) dried apricots, soaked overnight
2 eggs
200 ml (7 fl oz) natural yogurt
25 g (1 oz) soft brown sugar

Sift the flour, cocoa powder and drinking chocolate powder into a bowl. Rub in the margarine and lard or vegetable fat until the mixture resembles fine breadcrumbs. Add the water and mix to a firm dough. Turn on to a floured surface. Knead until smooth. Wrap in foil and chill in the refrigerator for 15 minutes.

Turn the dough on to a lightly floured surface. Roll out and use to line a 23 cm (9 inch) flan tin or dish, then prick the base.

To make the filling, drain the prunes and apricots. Remove the stones from the prunes and chop both fruits, then place in the flan case. In a bowl, beat the eggs with the yogurt and sugar and pour over the fruit. Bake in a preheated oven, 190°C (375°F), Gas Mark 5, for 30–40 minutes until the filling is set. Serve warm, sprinkled with grated chocolate and accompanied by Quick Chocolate Sauce (see page 19) or single cream.

Serves 6–8

Chocolate Apple Envelopes

50 g (2 oz) plain flour

40 g (1½ oz) wholemeal flour

25 g (1 oz) drinking chocolate powder

pinch of salt

1 egg, beaten

300 ml (½ pint) milk

Filling:

1 kg (2 lb) Bramley apples, peeled, cored and sliced

grated rind and juice of 1 orange

50 g (2 oz) granulated or caster sugar

1 tablespoon orange liqueur

To decorate:

white chocolate curls

fine strands of orange rind

Place the plain flour, wholemeal flour, drinking chocolate and salt in a bowl and make a well in the centre. Add the egg and half of the milk. Beat until smooth, then gradually stir in the remaining milk. Pour into a jug. Make 8 pancakes as described on page 11. Keep warm.

To make the filling, place the apples in a saucepan with the orange rind and juice and the sugar. Heat gently for 15 minutes until the apples are soft. Cool slightly, add the liqueur and beat to a pulp.

Divide the mixture among the warm pancakes and fold each one

left: apricot and prune tart, orange black magic pudding, chocolate apple envelopes
right: chocolate meringue pie

into 4. Decorate with white chocolate curls and orange rind. Serve with cream or natural yogurt.

Serves 4

Chocolate Meringue Pie

125 g (4 oz) plain flour

50 g (2 oz) margarine

15 g (½ oz) icing sugar, sifted

1 egg yolk

2 tablespoons water

Filling and topping:

25 g (1 oz) cornflour

2 eggs, separated

300 ml (½ pint) milk

125 g (4 oz) plain chocolate, broken into pieces

125 g (4 oz) caster sugar

Sift the flour into a bowl, and rub in the margarine. Stir in the icing sugar, then add the egg yolk and water and mix to a stiff dough. Turn on to a floured surface and knead until smooth. Wrap in foil and chill in the refrigerator for 30 minutes.

Roll out the pastry and use to line an 18 cm (7 inch) flan tin or dish. Prick the pastry base, line with greaseproof paper and cover with baking beans. Bake in a preheated oven, 190°C (375°F), Gas Mark 5, for 15 minutes. Remove the lining and beans and return the case to the oven for 5 minutes more.

To make the filling, mix together the cornflour and egg yolks. Heat the milk in a saucepan until almost boiling, then pour on to the egg-yolk mixture, stirring constantly. Return to the saucepan, add the chocolate and heat, stirring, until the chocolate melts and the sauce thickens. Continue to cook for 1 minute. Cool slightly then pour into the pastry case. Cover the surface with clingfilm or dampened greaseproof paper and set aside to cool completely.

Whisk the egg whites until stiff. Whisk in the sugar 1 tablespoonful at a time. Pipe on to the chocolate mixture and bake in a preheated oven, 190°C (375°F), Gas Mark 5, for 9–12 minutes until golden. Serve with cream or natural fromage frais.

Serves 4–6

Semolina Chocolate Soufflé

600 ml (1 pint) milk

50 g (2 oz) plain chocolate, chopped

3 tablespoons semolina

1–2 tablespoons caster sugar

1 egg, separated

grated nutmeg

Grease a 900 ml (1½ pint) soufflé dish. Place the milk and chocolate in a saucepan and heat, stirring, until the chocolate melts. Bring to the boil, then sprinkle the semolina over the milk. Lower the heat and cook slowly, stirring, until the mixture comes to the boil and thickens. Stir in the sugar and simmer for 2 minutes more. Cool slightly then beat in the egg yolk.

Whisk the egg white until stiff, then fold into the mixture, mixing well. Spoon the mixture into the soufflé dish and sprinkle with nutmeg. Bake in a preheated oven, 180°C (350°F), Gas Mark 4, for 20 minutes until risen. Serve hot.

Serves 4

French Pear Flan

125 g (4 oz) plain flour

20 g (¾ oz) cocoa powder

pinch of salt

50 g (2 oz) block margarine, cubed

50 g (2 oz) caster sugar

2 egg yolks

2 drops vanilla essence

Filling:

5 ripe pears, peeled, cored and sliced

1 tablespoon water

1 ripe banana, mashed

1 tablespoon icing sugar (optional)

Glaze:

3 tablespoons apricot jam

1 teaspoon lemon juice

Sift the flour, cocoa powder and salt on to a pastry board and make a well in the centre. Place the margarine, caster sugar, egg yolks and vanilla essence in the well. Using the fingertips of one hand work the ingredients in the well together, then quickly draw in the flour. Knead lightly until smooth. Wrap in foil and chill for 1 hour.

Place the dough on a lightly floured surface. Roll out and use to line a 20 cm (8 inch) flan tin or dish. Prick the base, line with greaseproof paper and cover with baking beans. Bake in a preheated oven, 190°C (375°F), Gas Mark 5, for 15 minutes. Remove the lining and beans and return the pastry case to the oven for 5 minutes more. Set aside.

To make the filling, heat the slices from 3 of the pears gently in a saucepan with the water until soft. Purée in a blender or food processor, then stir in the banana, and icing sugar, if using. Spoon into the pastry case. Arrange the remaining pear slices on top. Return to the oven and bake for 25 minutes.

To make the glaze, put the apricot jam and lemon juice in a saucepan. Bring to the boil over a low heat, then strain through a sieve into a clean pan. Boil until clear. Brush the glaze over the pears and allow the flan to cool. Serve with cream or Greek yogurt.

Serves 6

Orange and Banana Pudding

125 g (4 oz) sunflower margarine

125 g (4 oz) caster sugar

2 eggs

125 g (4 oz) self-raising flour, sifted

15 g (½ oz) cocoa powder, sifted

grated rind and juice of ½ orange

2 ripe bananas, sliced

To decorate:

1 ripe banana, sliced and sprinkled
  with lemon juice

fine strands of orange rind

Grease a 900 ml (1½ pint) pudding basin. Combine all the pudding ingredients except the bananas in a bowl and beat well for 3 minutes. Fold in the banana slices, then spoon the mixture into the pudding basin. Cover with greaseproof paper and tie securely.

Steam for 2 hours, topping up the steamer with water whenever necessary. Turn on to a serving plate and decorate with banana slices and fine strands of orange rind. Serve with Quick Chocolate Sauce (see page 19).

Serves 6

left: semolina chocolate soufflé, french pear flan
right: orange and banana pudding, banana pancakes

Banana Pancakes

125 g (4 oz) plain flour

pinch of salt

1 egg, beaten

300 ml (½ pint) milk

1 banana, sliced, to decorate

Filling:

2 large bananas

125 g (4 oz) skimmed milk soft
  cheese or curd cheese

125 g (4 oz) chocolate yogurt

Sift the flour and salt into a bowl and make a well in the centre. Add the egg and half of the milk. Beat until smooth, then gradually stir in the remaining milk. Pour into a jug.

Wipe an 18 cm (7 inch) non-stick frying pan with oil and place over a moderate heat for 30 seconds. Coat the base with a little batter and cook until the underside is lightly browned. Turn the pancake and cook the other side. Repeat to make 8 pancakes. Cool on a wire rack.

Mash the bananas well. Stir in the cheese and yogurt. Mix well, then divide the mixture between the pancakes. Roll up and arrange 2 on each individual plate. Decorate with banana slices. Serve with Chocolate Fudge Sauce (see page 25).

Serves 4

Chocolate Pineapple Princess

600 ml (1 pint) milk

75 g (3 oz) plain chocolate, broken into pieces

15 g (½ oz) butter

125 g (4 oz) fresh breadcrumbs

2 eggs, separated

1 x 250 g (8 oz) can pineapple pieces in natural juice, drained

125 g (4 oz) caster sugar

caster sugar, for dredging (optional)

Combine the milk, chocolate and butter in a saucepan. Heat until the chocolate has melted and the milk is almost boiling. Remove from the heat and stir in the breadcrumbs. Leave to stand for 10–15 minutes, then beat in the egg yolks.

Arrange the pineapple on the base of a 1.2 litre (2 pint) ovenproof dish, then pour the crumb mixture over the top. Bake in a preheated oven, 160°C (325°F), Gas Mark 3, for 40 minutes until set.

Whisk the egg whites until stiff. Whisk in half the sugar, then fold in the remainder. Spoon or pipe the meringue over the pudding. Dredge with extra caster sugar, if using, and return to the oven for 20–25 minutes until the meringue is crisp and golden. Serve with whipped cream or natural fromage frais.

Serves 4

Chocolate Jelly

125 g (4 oz) skimmed milk soft cheese or curd cheese

25 g (1 oz) caster sugar

6 tablespoons milk

75 g (3 oz) plain chocolate, melted

2 tablespoons water

2 teaspoons powdered gelatine

150 ml (¼ pint) whipping cream, whipped

white chocolate curls, to decorate

Dampen a 600 ml (1 pint) jelly mould. Beat the cheese until softened. Stir in the sugar and milk, add the chocolate and mix well.

Place the water in a small bowl and sprinkle the gelatine on top. Set aside for 2 minutes until spongy. Place the bowl in simmering water until the gelatine has melted. Stir thoroughly. Cool, then add to the chocolate mixture with the cream. Mix well, then spoon into the jelly mould. Leave in the refrigerator until set. Dip the mould briefly into hot water, then turn out on to a serving plate. Decorate with white chocolate curls.

Serves 4

Chocolate Ginger Trifle

6 teaspoons ginger preserve extra jam

6 trifle sponges, split in half

1 x 300 g (10 oz) can mandarin orange segments in natural juice

3 tablespoons orange liqueur

2 pieces stem ginger, chopped

25 g (1 oz) caster sugar

25 g (1 oz) cornflour

1 tablespoon cocoa powder

600 ml (1 pint) milk

2 egg yolks

To decorate:

150 ml (¼ pint) whipping cream, whipped

stem ginger, sliced

chocolate curls

Spread the jam over the sponges. Arrange on the base of a 1.2 litre (2 pint) trifle bowl. Drain the mandarins, reserving 4 tablespoons of the juice. Spoon the liqueur over the sponges with the reserved juice. Top with the fruit and ginger.

Heat the sugar, cornflour, cocoa powder and milk in a saucepan, whisking constantly, until smooth and thickened. Continue to cook, stirring, for 2 minutes. Cool slightly, then beat in the egg yolks. Set aside, stirring frequently, until cold. Spoon over the fruit.

Decorate with piped cream, stem ginger and chocolate curls.

Serves 6

Chocolate Orange Roulade

4 eggs, separated

175 g (6 oz) caster sugar

40 g (1½ oz) cocoa powder

icing sugar

Filling:

150 ml (¼ pint) double cream, whipped

150 g (5 oz) natural fromage frais

2 tablespoons icing sugar, sifted

finely grated rind of 1 orange

1 tablespoon orange liqueur

Grease and line a 30 x 20 cm (12 x 8 inch) Swiss roll tin. In a bowl, whisk the egg yolks and sugar until thick and creamy. Sift the cocoa powder over the mixture and fold in thoroughly. In another bowl, whisk the egg whites until stiff, then gently fold them into the chocolate mixture.

Spoon the mixture into the Swiss roll tin and level the surface. Bake in a preheated oven, 180°C (350°F), Gas Mark 4, for 25–30 minutes until firm. Cool for 5 minutes, then cover with a damp tea towel and leave to become completely cold.

Sift icing sugar over a large sheet of greaseproof paper. Invert the cake on to the paper and carefully peel off the lining paper.

To make the filling, fold the cream, fromage frais, icing sugar, orange rind and liqueur together. Spread over the cake, then roll up like a Swiss roll with the help of the greaseproof paper. (The cake may crack when rolled; this is quite normal.) Transfer to a serving dish, dust with more icing sugar if needed. Serve within 2 hours.

Serves 6–8

left: chocolate pineapple princess, chocolate jelly
above: chocolate ginger trifle, chocolate orange roulade

until the liqueur has been absorbed.

Carefully pour a little warm water into the jam jar in the centre of the souffle. Leave for 3–5 seconds, then lift out the jar.

Spoon the macaroon mixture into the hollow and top with the remaining curls. Carefully peel away the paper collar.

To decorate, pipe rosettes with the remaining cream and finish with candied coffee beans.

Serves 4

Soufflé Monte Carlo

4 large eggs, separated

75 g (3 oz) caster sugar

3 teaspoons instant coffee powder or granules

1 tablespoon hot water

150 ml (¼ pint) water

15 g (½ oz) powdered gelatine

450 ml (¾ pint) double cream, whipped

125 g (4 oz) plain chocolate curls

125 g (4 oz) ratafia biscuits or 4 large macaroons 12 cm (5 inches) in diameter, roughly broken

4 tablespoons Tia Maria

8 candied coffee beans, to decorate

Make a paper collar with a double thickness of greaseproof paper to stand 7 cm (3 inches) above the rim of a 15 cm (6 inch) soufflé dish. Secure with string or an elastic band.

Beat the egg yolks and sugar until light and creamy. Dissolve the coffee in the hot water and add to the mixture.

Pour the water into a small heatproof bowl and sprinkle the gelatine over the top. Set the bowl over a pan of water and heat gently, stirring, until the gelatine has dissolved. Stir into the mixture and chill for about 1 hour until on the point of setting.

Fold two-thirds of the cream into the mixture. Whisk the egg whites until they stand in soft peaks and carefully fold into the mixture.

Paint a 500 g (1 lb) jam jar with cooking oil and stand it in the centre of the soufflé dish. Carefully layer the soufflé mixture with three-quarters of the chocolate curls around the jar, ending with a layer of soufflé. Level the surface, then chill until set.

Place the ratafia biscuits or macaroons in a small bowl and spoon over the Tia Maria. Leave

Hot Liqueur Soufflé

caster sugar, for dusting

50 g (2 oz) butter

50 g (2 oz) plain flour

300 ml (½ pint) milk

75 g (3 oz) plain or white chocolate, broken into pieces

2 tablespoons crème de menthe

3 eggs, separated

50 g (2 oz) caster sugar

Sauce:

150 ml (¼ pint) double cream

50 g (2 oz) plain or white chocolate, broken into pieces

2 tablespoons crème de menthe

1 egg yolk

Butter an 18 cm (7 inch) soufflé dish and dust with the sugar.

Combine the butter, flour and milk in a medium saucepan. Stirring continuously, heat gently until boiling. Stir vigorously until a thick paste is formed. Cook for 2–3 minutes, still stirring.

Away from the heat, add the chocolate and stir until smooth and completely blended into the sauce. Beat in the crème de menthe and egg yolks.

Whisk the 4 egg whites until very stiff, then add the sugar. Whisk again until very stiff, then using a metal spoon, fold the chocolate sauce into the egg whites, taking care not to knock the air out of the whites. Pour the souffle mixture into the soufflé dish and bake in a preheated oven, 180°C (350°F), Gas Mark 4, for 45–50 minutes until well risen. Do not open the door during the cooking time otherwise the soufflé will collapse.

To make the sauce, pour the cream into a small saucepan and add the chocolate. Heat gently, stirring constantly, until the chocolate has melted and is thoroughly smooth. Do not boil. Stir in the crème de menthe and egg yolk. Pour into a jug.

To serve, dust the soufflé with icing sugar and take it directly from the oven to a heatproof mat on the table. The soufflé has about 3 minutes after it is taken from the oven before collapsing. Serve with the sauce.

Serves 4

Strawberry Cheesecake Boxes

1 egg
25 g (1 oz) caster sugar
25 g (1 oz) flour
1 tablespoon warm water
Filling:
150 ml (¼ pint) water
1 x 150 g (5 oz) packet strawberry jelly
juice of ½ lemon
250 g (8 oz) full fat soft cheese
300 ml (½ pint) whipping cream, whipped
2 tablespoons redcurrant jelly, warmed
To decorate:
150 g (5 oz) plain chocolate, melted
9 candy strawberries or fresh strawberries

Line the base of an 18 cm (7 inch) square cake tin with lightly greased greasepoof paper.

Whisk the egg and sugar until light and foamy and the whisk leaves a trail when lifted.

Gently fold in the flour and water with a metal spoon, then pour into the prepared tin. Bake in a preheated oven, 200°C (400°F), Gas Mark 6, for 10–12 minutes until well risen and lightly golden brown. Turn out the cake and peel off the paper. Cool on a wire rack. Re-line the tin with greaseproof paper.

To make the filling, heat the water, dissolve the jelly in it, then add the lemon juice. Chill for about 30 minutes until the mixture becomes syrupy.

Cream the cheese until smooth, then gradually add the jelly, beating well between each addition. Fold in two-thirds of the cream, then pour the mixture into the cake tin. Chill for about 2 hours until set.

Brush the sponge square with the redcurrant jelly, then unmould the cheesecake on to the sponge. Peel off the paper and trim if necessary.

For the decoration, draw a 30 cm (12 inch) square on greaseproof paper. With a palette knife, spread the chocolate to fill the square. Cool until set. Cut the chocolate into 36 equal squares, then cut the cheesecake into 9 x 5 cm (2 inch) squares, trimming the edges if necessary. Working quickly to avoid over-handling the chocolate, press a piece of chocolate on to the 4 sides of each cheesecake square.

Fit a piping bag with a star nozzle, spoon in the remaining cream and pipe a ribbon on top of each cheesecake using a zig-zag motion. Decorate each with a strawberry.

Makes 9

Mandarin Yogurt Dessert

1 x 300 g (10 oz) can mandarin
  orange segments in natural juice,
  drained, juice reserved
caster sugar, to taste
15 g (½ oz) powdered gelatine
125 g (4 oz) plain chocolate
250 ml (8 fl oz) plain yogurt
2 tablespoons orange liqueur
  (optional)
To decorate (optional):
50 ml (2 fl oz) whipping cream,
  whipped
chocolate leaf

Pour the juice from the mandarin
oranges into a small saucepan. Add
sugar, to taste. Sprinkle the gelatine
over the juice and heat gently,
without boiling, until dissolved.

Break 75 g (3 oz) of the chocolate
into pieces and place in a heatproof
bowl. Set the bowl over a pan of hot
water and heat gently, stirring until
melted. Gradually stir in the yogurt,
beating vigorously until smooth.
Stir in the fruit juice. Reserve
1 orange segment. Roughly chop
the remainder and add to the bowl.

Grate the remaining chocolate
and add to the mixture, together
with the liqueur, if using. Pour into
a 600 ml (1 pint) decorative mould

and chill for about 3 hours until set.

Unmould the pudding and
decorate with cream, the reserved
orange segment and a chocolate
leaf, if liked.

Serves 4

Pear Upside-down Pudding

50 g (2 oz) butter
50 g (2 oz) dark brown sugar
1 x 875 g (1 ¾ lb) can pear halves,
  drained
8–10 whole glacé cherries
125 g (4 oz) margarine
125 g (4 oz) caster sugar
2 eggs
125 g (4 oz) self-raising flour, sifted
25 g (1 oz) cocoa powder, sifted
flaked almonds, to decorate
  (optional)

Heat the butter and brown sugar
gently until melted, then pour into
the base of an 18 cm (7 inch) deep
cake tin with a fixed base. Spread
evenly over the base.

Arrange the pears, rounded side
up, on the base of the tin. The
number that will fit on the base will
depend on the size of the pear
halves. Slide a whole glacé cherry
into the cavity under each pear half.
Chop the remaining pear halves.

Cream the margarine and sugar.
Beat in the eggs, one at a time, then
fold in the flour and cocoa.

Add the chopped pears to the mixture. Stir well, then carefully spoon over the pears in the tin. Gently level the mixture.

Bake in a preheated oven, 180°C (350°F), Gas Mark 4, for about 35 minutes until well risen and springy to the touch. Invert on to a serving dish. Decorate with flaked almonds, if using. Serve hot with a pouring custard or single cream.

Serves 6–8

left: pear upside-down pudding, mandarin yogurt dessert
right: chocolate fruit and nut flan

Chocolate Fruit and Nut Flan

175 g (6 oz) plain flour
pinch of salt
40 g (1½ oz) margarine
40 g (1½ oz) lard
1½ tablespoons water
Filling:
2 eggs
50 g (2 oz) caster sugar
125 g (4 oz) mixed nuts, chopped
125 g (4 oz) mixed dried fruit
50 g (2 oz) fresh breadcrumbs
1 tablespoon lemon juice
1 tablespoon rum
Topping:
125 g (4 oz) plain chocolate, melted

Sift the flour and salt into a bowl. Rub in the margarine and lard until the mixture resembles fine breadcrumbs. Add the water and mix to a firm dough. Turn on to a lightly floured surface and knead until smooth. Roll out the pastry and use to line a 20–23 cm (8–9 inch) flan tin or dish, then prick the base.

To make the filling, put the eggs and sugar in a bowl and whisk until pale and thick. Stir in the nuts, mixed dried fruit, breadcrumbs, lemon juice and rum, then mix well. Spoon the mixture into the pastry case, place the tin or dish on a baking sheet, and bake in a preheated oven, 190°C (375°F), Gas Mark 5, for 25–30 minutes until set and golden.

Allow the flan to cool, then spread the chocolate over the top. Leave to set. Serve with natural fromage frais.

Serves 6–8

Banana Bavarois

½ x 150 g (5 oz) packet lemon jelly
250 ml (8 fl oz) hot water
2 small bananas, thinly sliced
Bavarois:
2 eggs, separated
2 tablespoons sugar
grated rind of ½ lemon
½ teaspoon vanilla essence
150 ml (¼ pint) milk
2 teaspoons powdered gelatine
300 ml (½ pint) whipping cream,
   whipped
125 g (4 oz) plain chocolate, broken
   into pieces, melted

Dissolve the jelly in the hot water, then pour in sufficient jelly to cover the base of a 500 g (1 lb) loaf tin. Chill until set.

Toss the banana slices in the remaining jelly. Strain, and reserve the jelly. Stand the loaf tin in a bowl of warm water, to prevent the jelly setting. Position the banana slices in the jelly, slightly overlapping, in 3–4 rows running the length of the loaf tin. Leave to set, then spoon over the liquid jelly.

To make the bavarois, beat the egg yolks, sugar, lemon rind and

vanilla essence until light and creamy. Heat the milk until just boiling, then pour over the egg-yolk mixture. Return to the rinsed pan and heat gently, without boiling, for about 10 minutes until the mixture is thick enough to coat the back of a wooden spoon. Remove from the heat. Whisking the bavarois with a fork, gradually sprinkle in the gelatine and stir until dissolved. Cool, then chill for about 1 hour until on the point of setting.

Fold half the cream into the bavarois mixture. Whisk the egg whites until stiff peaks form, then fold into the mixture. Pour into the tin and chill for 3 hours until set. Unmould on to a serving dish.

Using a palette knife, coat the sides with a thin layer of the remaining cream.

Draw a 20 x 30 cm (8 x 12 inch) rectangle on a piece of greaseproof paper and, using a palette knife, spread the melted chocolate over the rectangle. Leave in a cool place until set.

Cut the chocolate into 5 x 2.5 cm (2 x 1 inch) rectangles and place them overlapping, with the longest side vertical, all the way around the bavarois, pressing them gently against the cream. Decorate with rosettes, using the remaining cream.

Serves 4

right: profiteroles with chocolate sauce, truffle jalousie
left: banana bavarois

Truffle Jalousie

250 g (8 oz) Madeira cake, crumbled
125 g (4 oz) almonds, chopped and
   toasted
5 tablespoons cocoa powder
50 g (2 oz) butter, softened
4 tablespoons mincemeat
1 egg
250 g (8 oz) puff pastry
milk or water, for brushing
icing sugar, for dusting

Grease a baking sheet. Combine the cake crumbs, almonds, cocoa, butter, mincemeat and egg in a bowl and beat until mixed.

Roll out the puff pastry on a lightly floured surface and trim to a 28 x 33 cm (11 x 13 inches) oblong. With the blunt side of a knife, mark a line 7 cm (3 inches) in from each long edge. With a sharp knife, cut 1 cm (½ inch) strips on the slant from the mark to the edge of the pastry. Spread the filling down the centre of the pastry leaving a 1 cm (½ inch) gap between the filling and the cuts in the pastry. Lightly brush the pastry surrounding the filling with milk or water. To seal the ends, fold the 2 short ends about 2.5 cm (1 inch) over the filling. Place the pastry strips alternately from each side over the filling to form a plait. Press down lightly. Using a large slice or spatula, carefully lift the plait on to the greased baking sheet and bake in a preheated oven, 220°C (425°F), Gas Mark 7, for 20 minutes until the pastry is well risen and pale golden brown.

Sprinkle the plait generously with icing sugar and return to the oven for 5 minutes until the sugar has melted to a shiny glaze. Remove immediately and cool on a wire rack. Serve cold cut into fingers.

Serves 4

Profiteroles with Chocolate Sauce

Choux Pastry:

150 ml (¼ pint) water

50 g (2 oz) butter

65 g (2½ oz) plain flour, sifted

2 eggs

Filling:

2 tablespoons instant custard powder

1 tablespoon cocoa powder

1 tablespoon sugar

300 ml (½ pint) milk

150 ml (¼ pint) double cream, whipped

Quick Chocolate Sauce:

2 tablespoons cocoa powder

4 tablespoons golden syrup

50 g (2 oz) chilled butter, diced

150 ml (¼ pint) milk

½ teaspoon vanilla essence

Sprinkle 2 large baking sheets with a little cold water; this helps the choux balls to rise.

To make the choux pastry, first heat the water and butter in a pan. When the butter has melted, bring to the boil. Remove from the heat and add the flour. Beat vigorously with a wooden spoon until the paste leaves the sides of the pan and forms a smooth ball. Cool slightly.

Beat in the eggs, 1 at a time, until the mixture becomes smooth and glossy. Fill a large piping bag fitted with a large plain nozzle with the choux pastry, and pipe about 24 equal-sized balls on to the baking sheets. Bake in a preheated oven, 200°C (400°F), Gas Mark 6, for about 30 minutes until well risen and golden brown. Quickly split each choux ball with a knife and return to the oven for a few minutes to dry out.

To make the filling, blend the custard powder, cocoa and sugar with a little of the milk. Bring the remaining milk to the boil. Pour over the custard, stir well and return to the rinsed pan. Return to the boil, stirring constantly and cook for 2–3 minutes. Tip into a clean bowl to cool. Cover closely with clingfilm or dampened greaseproof paper to prevent a skin forming.

In a blender, mix the custard and cream together until smooth. Fit a large piping bag fitted with a large plain nozzle, spoon in the cream mixture and fill each choux bun.

Blend all the chocolate sauce ingredients in a small pan. Heat until smooth and melted, stirring constantly. Bring to the boil and cook gently for 2–3 minutes.

Place the filled buns on a large serving dish. Pour over a little of the sauce and serve the rest separately.

Serves 4

Chocolate Cream Pie

125 g (4 oz) plain or white chocolate
50 ml (2 fl oz) water
2 teaspoons powdered gelatine
150 ml (¼ pint) single cream
icing sugar, to decorate (optional)
Pastry:
25 g (1 oz) caster sugar
40 g (1½ oz) butter
2 eggs, separated
65 g (2½ oz) plain flour

To make the pastry, cream the sugar and butter until light and fluffy, then beat in 1 egg yolk. Gradually work in the flour to a soft, pliable dough. Knead lightly on a floured surface until smooth.

Roll out the pastry and use to line a 15 cm (6 inch) fluted flan ring. Prick the base with a fork and leave for 30 minutes.

Grease a piece of foil to fit the flan ring and gently press the greased side of the foil over the pastry case. Bake in a preheated oven, 200°C (400°F), Gas Mark 6, for 15–20 minutes until crisp and lightly coloured. Remove the foil for the last 5 minutes of cooking. Unmould and cool on a wire rack.

Reserve 1 square of chocolate and break the remainder into small pieces. Put in a small heatproof bowl. Set the bowl over a saucepan of hot water until melted, stirring until smooth. Remove the bowl from the heat and beat in the remaining egg yolk.

Pour the water into a small heatproof bowl and sprinkle over the gelatine. Set the bowl over a pan of hot water and heat until the gelatine has dissolved. Stir into the chocolate mixture, then stir in the cream. Cool until on the point of setting.

Whisk the egg whites until standing in soft peaks, then gently fold into the chocolate cream. Chill for about 2 hours until set.

Just before serving, pile the chocolate cream into the pastry case and grate over the reserved chocolate. Dust with icing sugar, if using. Serve within 2 hours, or the pastry will start to soften.

Serves 4

Apricot Chocolate Cheesecake

1 x 200 g (7 oz) chocolate Swiss roll, cut into 1 cm (½ inch) slices

2 x 425 g (14 oz) cans apricot halves, drained and 4 tablespoons juice reserved

500 g (1 lb) curd cheese

3 tablespoons caster sugar

juice of ½ lemon

2 eggs, separated

15 g (½ oz) powdered gelatine

150 ml (¼ pint) whipping cream, whipped

To decorate:

15 g (½ oz) plain chocolate

15 g (½ oz) butter or margarine

65 ml (2½ fl oz) double or whipping cream, whipped (optional)

Line the base of a 1.2 litre (2 pint) glass serving dish with the Swiss roll slices.

Reserve 4 apricot halves and purée the remainder.

In a large bowl, blend the curd cheese, sugar and lemon juice together, then gradually stir in the apricot purée. The resulting mixture should be smooth and runny. Beat in the egg yolks.

Place the reserved apricot juice in a small heatproof bowl and sprinkle over the gelatine. Set the bowl over a pan of hot water and stir until the gelatine has dissolved. Blend into the cheesecake mixture and chill for about 1 hour until on the point of setting.

Fold the cream into the cheesecake mixture. Whisk the egg whites until standing in soft peaks and carefully fold into the mixture. Pour the cheesecake mixture over the Swiss roll slices and level with a spatula.

To decorate, melt the chocolate and butter in a small heatpoof bowl set over a pan of hot water. Stir until smooth.

Fill a small greaseproof paper piping bag with the chocolate mixture and pipe parallel lines about 2.5 cm (1 inch) apart over the surface of the cheesecake. Turn the cheesecake through 45° so the chocolate lines run horizontally, then draw the point of a sharp knife down across the lines about 2.5 cm (1 inch) apart. Turn the cheesecake through 180° and draw the knife across the chocolate lines in the opposite direction to produce a feathered effect.

Decorate with rosettes of cream, if using. Halve each reserved apricot, cut into a small fan shape and place on the cheesecake.

Serves 6–8

left: chocolate cream pie, apricot chocolate cheesecake, hot chocolate trifle

Hot Chocolate Trifle

1 x 200 g (7 oz) Swiss roll with vanilla filling, cut into 1 cm (½ inch) slices

25 g (1 oz) plain chocolate, cut into small pieces

4 tablespoons medium sherry

300 ml (½ pint) milk

2 eggs

1 egg yolk

1 tablespoon caster sugar

few drops vanilla essence

To decorate:

25 g (1 oz) walnuts, chopped

25 g (1 oz) glacé cherries, chopped

Lightly grease a 600 ml (1 pint) ovenproof clear bowl or soufflé dish. Line the base and side with some of the Swiss roll slices.

Cube the remaining slices and layer with the chocolate in the bowl or dish. Spoon the sherry over the Swiss roll and chocolate.

Warm the milk. Beat the remaining ingredients together, then pour over the milk and mix.

Strain the custard on to the Swiss roll and chocolate and leave to stand for 30 minutes.

Put the bowl or dish in a roasting tin and pour 900 ml (1½ pints) water around it. Bake in a preheated oven, 180°C (350°F), Gas Mark 4, for 1 hour until the custard is set.

Sprinkle with the walnuts and glacé cherries just before serving.

Serves 4

Quick Chocolate Mousse

1 teaspoon instant coffee powder or
  granules
1 tablespoon hot water
2 teaspoons orange liqueur
150 g (5 oz) plain chocolate, melted
4 eggs, separated

To decorate:
50 ml (2 fl oz) whipping cream,
  whipped
4 chocolate leaves

Blend the instant coffee with the water and liqueur, and add to the chocolate. Stir until smooth.

Stir in the egg yolks.

Whisk the egg whites until stiff and fold carefully but thoroughly into the chocolate mixture.

Divide the mixture among individual ramekin dishes or glass bowls and chill for at least 2 hours or overnight.

Just before serving, pipe a rosette of cream on each mousse and decorate with a chocolate leaf.

Serves 4

Iced Rum and Raisin Mousse

75 g (3 oz) seedless raisins
4 tablespoons rum
125 g (4 oz) plain chocolate, melted
2 eggs, separated
300 ml (½ pint) double cream,
  whipped
To decorate:
65 ml (2½ fl oz) double cream,
  whipped
8 chocolate cut-out shapes (optional)

Place the raisins in a small bowl and pour over the rum. Leave to stand for at least 8 hours or overnight.

Stir the chocolate and egg yolks together, then add the raisins and rum. Fold in the cream.

Whisk the egg whites until standing in soft peaks, then fold into the mixture.

Transfer to a 600 ml (1 pint) freezerproof serving dish and place in the freezer for about 2 hours until just firm throughout.

Stand the mousse in the refrigerator for 15 minutes before serving.

Decorate with a border of cream, and chocolate shapes, if using.

Serves 4

left: chocolate bread and butter pudding, chocolate heart, iced rum and raisin mousse

Chocolate Bread and Butter Pudding

4 slices of bread from a large loaf,
  crusts removed
25 g (1 oz) butter, softened
1 teaspoon ground cinnamon
40 g (1½ oz) sugar
3 eggs
600 ml (1 pint) milk
1 teaspoon instant coffee powder or
  granules
75 g (3 oz) plain chocolate, grated

Lightly grease a 900 ml (1½ pint) pie dish. Spread the butter over the bread. Sprinkle with the cinnamon. Cut each slice into 4 triangles.

Beat the sugar and eggs together in a bowl. Heat the milk, coffee and half of the chocolate to lukewarm. Whisk until well blended, then pour over the egg mixture. Mix well.

Layer the bread in the pie dish and strain the custard over the top. Let stand for 30 minutes.

Put the dish in a roasting tin and pour about 900 ml (1½ pints) water around it. Bake in a preheated oven, 180°C (350°F), Gas Mark 4, for 1¼–1½ hours until the custard is set. Ten minutes before the end of the cooking time, sprinkle over the remaining chocolate.

Serves 4

Chocolate Hearts

250 g (8 oz) low-fat soft cream
  cheese, sifted if necessary
75 g (3 oz) plain chocolate, melted
1 tablespoon caster sugar
grated rind and juice of 1 orange
1 teaspoon powdered gelatine
65 ml (2½ fl oz) whipping cream,
  whipped
1 quantity Quick Chocolate Sauce (see
  page 19) or 150 ml (¼ pint) single
  cream, to serve
chocolate cut-out shapes, to decorate

Line 4 heart-shaped moulds with muslin. Gradually spoon the cheese into the chocolate, beating well between each addition. Add the sugar and orange rind.

Place the orange juice in a small, heatproof bowl and sprinkle over the gelatine. Set the bowl over a pan of hot water and stir until dissolved. Cool slightly; add to the cheese mixture. Chill for about 30 minutes until on the point of setting.

Fold the mixture into the cream. Divide equally among the moulds. Level the surface and chill for about 2 hours until set.

Carefully unmould the hearts on to a serving dish and peel off the muslin. Coat each heart with chocolate sauce or cream, and decorate with a chocolate shape. Serve with fresh orange segments.

Serves 4

Ice Creams

Iced Chocolate Orange Soufflé

4 eggs, separated
125 g (4 oz) caster sugar
grated rind and juice of 1 orange
1 tablespoon drinking chocolate
   powder
50 g (2 oz) plain chocolate, melted
300 ml (½ pint) double cream,
   whipped
To decorate:
chocolate leaves
fine strands of orange rind

Tie a double band of foil or
greaseproof paper tightly around a
600 ml (1 pint) soufflé dish to stand
5 cm (2 inches) above the rim.

   Place the egg yolks, sugar and
orange rind in a bowl and whisk
until pale and thick. In a cup, mix
the drinking chocolate to a paste
with the orange juice and stir into
the melted chocolate. Whisk into
the egg mixture. Whisk the egg
whites until stiff, then fold into the
mixture with the cream. Pour into
the dish and freeze until firm.

   Carefully remove the paper and
put the soufflé in the refrigerator
15 minutes before serving to soften
slightly. Decorate with chocolate
leaves and orange rind.

Serves 4–6

Chocolate Mint Ice Cream

125 g (4 oz) white chocolate, broken
  into pieces
65 ml (2½ fl oz) single cream
300 ml (½ pint) double cream,
  whipped
40 g (1½ oz) icing sugar, sifted
½ teaspoon peppermint essence
25 g (1 oz) chocolate mint sticks,
  chopped
green food colouring
chocolate mint sticks, to serve
  (optional)

Place the chocolate and single cream in a heatproof bowl and set over a saucepan of gently simmering water. Stir until the chocolate has melted.

In a large bowl, blend a little of the double cream with the chocolate mixture. Stir in the icing sugar, then combine with the remaining cream. Stir in the peppermint essence, chocolate mint sticks and enough colouring to tint the mixture green. Spoon into a rigid container. Freeze for 2 hours, then transfer to a bowl and beat until smooth. Return to the rinsed container and freeze until firm.

Transfer the ice cream to the refrigerator 15 minutes before serving to soften slightly. Serve at once in individual dishes, with chocolate mint sticks, if using.

Serves 4–6

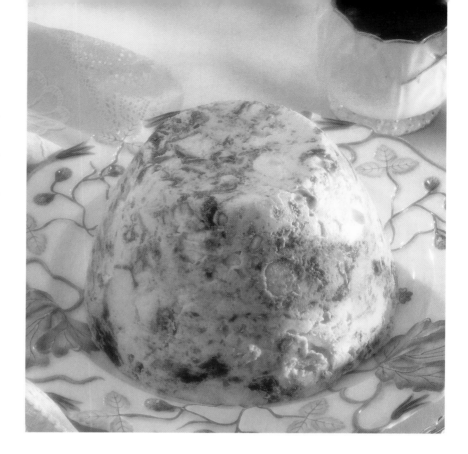

Chocolate Bombe

300 ml (½ pint) double cream
65 ml (2½ fl oz) single cream
125 g (4 oz) plain chocolate, melted
1–2 tablespoons rum
125 g (4 oz) meringues (see page 46),
  crumbled
Chocolate Fudge Sauce:
50 g (2 oz) butter
25 g (1 oz) soft brown sugar
1½ tablespoons milk
50 g (2 oz) plain chocolate, broken
  into pieces

Combine the double and single creams in a bowl and whip. Blend a little of the whipped cream with the chocolate, then stir in the rum.

Add the meringues to the remaining cream and mix well. Add the chocolate mixture, swirling it through to give a marbled effect. Spoon into a 1.2 litre (2 pint) pudding basin, cover with a lid or foil and freeze until firm.

To make the chocolate fudge sauce, put all the ingredients in a nonstick saucepan and heat gently, stirring occasionally, until smooth and hot.

Quickly dip the basin in hot water then invert the chocolate bombe on to a serving plate. Put in the refrigerator for 20–25 minutes before serving to soften slightly. Serve with the chocolate fudge sauce in a separate jug.

Serves 6

*Left: iced chocolate orange soufflé,
chocolate mint ice cream
right: chocolate bombe*

Apricot and Chocolate Iced Loaf

1 x 411 g (13½ oz) can apricot halves
  in fruit juice
2 eggs, separated
125 g (4 oz) caster sugar
300 ml (½ pint) whipping cream,
  whipped
50 g (2 oz) skimmed milk soft cheese
  or curd cheese
65 ml (2½ fl oz) whipping cream
125 g (4 oz) plain chocolate, melted
To decorate:
65 ml (2½ fl oz) whipping cream,
  whipped
chocolate triangles

Drain and discard most of the juice from the can of apricots, then place the fruit and remaining juice in a blender or food processor. Process to a purée and set aside.

Place the egg yolks in a bowl with 50 g (2 oz) of the caster sugar and whisk until pale and thick. In a second bowl, whisk the egg whites until they are stiff, then whisk in the remaining caster sugar, 1 tablespoonful at a time. Fold into the egg yolk mixture and mix thoroughly. Carefully fold in the whipped cream and the prepared apricot purée.

Spoon the mixture into a rigid freezer container and freeze for about 4 hours until just firm.

Meanwhile, beat the cheese with the 65 ml (2½ fl oz) whipping cream in a bowl. Add the chocolate and mix well. Set aside.

Grease a 1 kg (2 lb) loaf tin. Turn the apricot ice cream into a bowl and beat until smooth. Place one-third of the mixture in the loaf tin. Drop about half of the chocolate mixture in spoonfuls over the ice cream. Top with half the remaining ice cream, then drop the remaining chocolate mixture in spoonfuls on top. Finish the loaf by spreading ice cream lightly over the surface. Cover and freeze until firm.

About 15 minutes before serving, turn the loaf on to a serving plate and decorate with piped cream and chocolate triangles. Place in the refrigerator until required.

Serves 8–10

Chocolate Ice Cream

2 eggs, separated
65 ml (2½ fl oz) double cream
50 g (2 oz) caster sugar
1 x 200 g (7 oz) can evaporated milk, chilled
125 g (4 oz) plain chocolate, melted

In a bowl, combine the egg yolks and double cream, mix well and set aside. In a large bowl, whisk the egg whites until stiff, then whisk in the sugar, 1 tablespoonful at a time. Whisk the egg-yolk mixture into the egg-white mixture.

Pour the evaporated milk into a bowl and whisk until thick. Fold into the egg mixture. Blend a little of the mixture with the chocolate, then stir into the egg and evaporated milk mixture. Mix well and spoon into a rigid container. Freeze until firm.

Transfer the ice cream to the refrigerator 15 minutes before serving to soften slightly. Serve on its own or with fresh fruit, Quick Chocolate Sauce (see page 19) or biscuits.

Serves 4–6

Mocha Ice Cream

2 teaspoons instant coffee granules
150 ml (¼ pint) milk
50 g (2 oz) plain chocolate, melted in a large bowl
1 egg white
50 g (2 oz) caster sugar
75 ml (3 fl oz) whipping cream, whipped
25 g (1 oz) walnuts, finely chopped
chopped walnuts, to decorate

Place the coffee granules and milk in a saucepan and heat until almost boiling. Gradually pour on to the chocolate, mixing well, then set the mocha mixture aside to cool.

In a bowl, whisk the egg white until stiff, then whisk in the sugar, 1 tablespoonful at a time. Fold into the mocha mixture with the cream and walnuts.

Pour into a rigid container, cover and freeze until firm. Remove from the freezer 5 minutes before serving and leave at room temperature to soften slightly before spooning into individual bowls. Decorate with chopped walnuts.

Serves 4

Mini Chocolate Castles

50 g (2 oz) plain chocolate, melted
1 tablespoon cocoa powder
1 tablespoon boiling water
1 tablespoon brandy
1 egg white
50 g (2 oz) caster sugar
150 ml (¼ pint) whipping cream, lightly whipped
white chocolate curls, to decorate

Chill 4 ramekins in the freezer for 5 minutes; pour one-quarter of the chocolate into each ramekin and rotate to cover the bases completely.

Mix the cocoa powder to a paste with the water. Stir in the brandy.

Whisk the egg white until stiff; whisk in the sugar, 1 tablespoonful at a time. Blend the cream and the cooled cocoa and brandy mixture. Fold in the egg white and mix lightly but thoroughly. Divide among the 4 ramekins. Cover with foil and freeze until firm.

Quickly dip the ramekins into hot water, then invert on to individual serving plates. Decorate with white chocolate curls.

Serves 4

left: chocolate ice cream, mocha ice cream, apricot and chocolate iced loaf
right: mini chocolate castles

Rhubarb and Chocolate Ice Cream

500 g (1 lb) rhubarb, sliced
125 g (4 oz) caster sugar
2 tablespoons water
2 egg whites
75 g (3 oz) icing sugar
150 ml (¼ pint) double cream,
    whipped
75 g (3 oz) plain chocolate, broken
    into pieces and melted

Put the rhubarb, sugar and water in a large saucepan and cook gently for 15 minutes until the fruit is soft. Cool slightly, then purée in a blender or food processor. Transfer the fruit purée to a large bowl and set aside.

In a bowl, whisk the egg whites until they are stiff, then whisk in the icing sugar, 1 tablespoonful at a time. Fold into the rhubarb purée along with the double cream and melted chocolate. Spoon into a rigid freezer container, cover and freeze until firm.

Transfer the ice cream to the refrigerator 15 minutes before serving to soften slightly. Spoon into individual dishes to serve.

Serves 6

Chocolate Maple Ice Cream

50 g (2 oz) raisins
4 tablespoons boiling water
2 egg yolks
50 g (2 oz) soft brown sugar
50 g (2 oz) plain chocolate, broken
    into pieces
3 tablespoons maple syrup
300 ml (½ pint) double cream,
    whipped

Place the raisins in a bowl and add the measured boiling water. Leave to soak for 15 minutes, then drain and set aside.

In a large bowl, whisk the egg yolks and sugar together until thick and pale. Combine the chocolate and maple syrup in a heatproof bowl and set over a saucepan of gently simmering water. Stir until the chocolate has melted. Allow to cool, then combine with the egg-mixture and fold in the cream. Spoon into a rigid container, cover and freeze for 1–2 hours.

Spoon the ice cream into a bowl and beat until smooth, then fold in the raisins. Return to the rinsed container, cover and freeze until the ice cream is firm.

Transfer the ice cream to the refrigerator 15 minutes before serving to soften slightly. Serve with langues de chat or Viennese Chocolate Whirls (see page 87).

Serves 4–6

Speckled Mango Ice Cream

2 mangoes
2 tablespoons lemon juice
2 egg whites
50 g (2 oz) caster sugar
150 ml (¼ pint) whipping cream,
   whipped
1 large chocolate flake bar, crushed
25 g (1 oz) plain chocolate, chopped

Cut the mangoes in half, remove the stones and scoop out the flesh. Purée with the lemon juice in a blender or food processor, transfer to a large bowl and set aside.

In a second bowl, whisk the egg whites until stiff, then whisk in the sugar, 1 tablespoonful at a time. Fold into the mango purée with the cream, chocolate flake and chocolate. Mix well, then spoon into a rigid container, cover and freeze until firm.

Transfer the ice cream to the refrigerator 15 minutes before serving to soften slightly. Scoop into individual glass bowls and serve with a fruit salad or Quick Chocolate Sauce (see page 19).

Serves 6

left: rhubarb and chocolate ice cream, chocolate maple ice cream
right: speckled mango ice cream

Chocolate Fruit

1 x 411 g (13½ oz) can peaches in
    fruit juice, drained
4 scoops Chocolate Ice Cream (see
    page 27)
½ quantity Quick Chocolate Sauce
    (see page 19)
150 ml (¼ pint) whipping cream,
    whipped
chocolate curls, to decorate

Divide half the peaches among
4 tall sundae glasses. Add a scoop of
chocolate ice cream to each, then
top with the remaining fruit.

Pour the sauce over, then pipe
large whirls of cream on top.
Decorate with chocolate curls and
serve at once.

Serves 4

Tipsy Christmas Bombe

25 g (1 oz) raisins
25 g (1 oz) glacé cherries, chopped
50 g (2 oz) mixed dried fruit
3 tablespoons rum
3 tablespoons sherry
450 ml (¾ pint) single cream
3 egg yolks
75 g (3 oz) soft brown sugar
125 g (4 oz) plain chocolate, melted
finely grated rind of 1 orange
150 ml (¼ pint) double cream,
    whipped

Combine the raisins, glacé cherries
and mixed dried fruit in a bowl.
Add the rum and sherry, stir, and
leave to soak for 4 hours or
overnight.

Heat the single cream gently to
simmering point. Place the egg
yolks in a large bowl with the sugar
and whisk until thick and pale. Add
the hot cream, stirring constantly,
then strain the mixture back into
the clean saucepan.

Heat gently, stirring until the
mixture thickens and coats the back
of a spoon. Cover the surface with
clingfilm or damp greaseproof paper
and leave to cool. Gently fold in the
chocolate, orange rind and double
cream, then mix lightly but
thoroughly.

Transfer to a rigid container, cover
and freeze for 1 hour. Spoon into a
bowl and beat the mixture until
smooth. Return to the rinsed
container, cover and freeze again.
Repeat after 1 hour, then fold in the
fruit, transfer to a 900 ml (1½ pint)
pudding basin, cover and freeze
until the ice cream is firm.

Transfer the ice cream to the
refrigerator 15 minutes before
serving to soften slightly. Quickly
dip the basin into hot water, then
invert the bombe on to a serving
plate and serve immediately.

Serves 6

right: chocolate fruit, tipsy christmas bombe, edwardian rum ice cream

Edwardian Rum Ice Cream

50 g (2 oz) wholemeal breadcrumbs
25 g (1 oz) walnuts, finely chopped
50 g (2 oz) soft brown sugar
1 egg, separated
150 ml (¼ pint) natural yogurt
40 g (1½ oz) plain chocolate, grated
1 tablespoon rum or 1 teaspoon rum
    flavouring

Line a baking sheet with foil. In a
small bowl, combine the
breadcrumbs, walnuts and 25 g
(1 oz) of the sugar. Mix well, then
spread over the foil. Put under a
preheated grill for 2 minutes until
the mixture is toasted and golden.
Allow to cool.

Whisk the egg white in a bowl
until stiff, then whisk in the
remaining sugar.

In another bowl, mix the egg yolk
with the yogurt, then stir in the
toasted crumb mixture and grated
chocolate. Fold in the egg-white
mixture with the rum or rum
flavouring and spoon into a rigid
container. Freeze until firm.

Transfer the ice cream to the
refrigerator 15 minutes before
serving to allow it to soften slightly.
Spoon into bowls and serve with a
jug of Quick Chocolate Sauce (see
page 19).

Serves 4

Gâteaux and Cheesecakes

Black Forest Gâteau

3 eggs

75 g (3 oz) caster sugar

75 g (3 oz) plain flour

1½ tablespoons cocoa powder

1½ teaspoons baking powder

2 tablespoons hot water

Filling and decoration:

150 ml (¼ pint) double cream

65 ml (2½ fl oz) single cream

1½ tablespoons kirsch

1 x 425 g (14 oz) can cherry pie filling

25 g (1 oz) plain chocolate, grated

Grease and base-line 2 x 18 cm (7 inch) sandwich tins. In a bowl, whisk the eggs with the sugar until the mixture is pale and thick and the whisk leaves a trail. Sift the flour, cocoa and baking powder, then fold into the egg mixture with the water.

Divide the cake mixture between the tins. Bake in a preheated oven, 190°C (375°F), Gas Mark 5, for 20 minutes until risen and firm. Invert on to a wire rack to cool.

Combine the double and single creams in a bowl and whisk until stiff. Place 1 cake on a board and spoon over half the kirsch. Spoon one-third of the cream into a piping bag and pipe a border around the edge of the cake.

Reserve 6 cherries for decoration. Remove most of the sauce from the remaining cherries. Spoon the fruit inside the band of cream. Spoon the rest of the kirsch over the other cake and place on top of the cherries. Spread the cake top and side with some of the remaining cream and sprinkle with grated chocolate. Pipe on the rest of the cream and decorate with the reserved cherries.

Serves 6–8

Mocha Cheesecake

50 g (2 oz) butter, melted

125 g (4 oz) bourbon biscuits, crushed

Filling:

250 g (8 oz) carton skimmed milk soft cheese or curd cheese

2 eggs, separated

50 g (2 oz) caster sugar

150 ml (¼ pint) single cream

2 teaspoons instant coffee granules

4 tablespoons hot water

15 g (½ oz) powdered gelatine

75 g (3 oz) plain chocolate, melted

Topping:

whole hazelnuts

25 g (1 oz) plain chocolate, melted

65 ml (2½ fl oz) double cream, whipped

Grease a 20 cm (8 inch) loose-bottomed cake tin. Mix the butter with the biscuit crumbs in a bowl. Press on to the base of the cake tin. Leave in a cool place to set.

Meanwhile, make the filling. Place the cheese in a large bowl, beat to soften slightly, then beat in the egg yolks, sugar and single cream. Dissolve the coffee granules in the hot water in a small bowl and leave to cool.

Sprinkle the gelatine over the surface of the cold coffee. Set aside for 2 minutes until spongy. Place the bowl over a saucepan of simmering water until the gelatine has melted. Stir thoroughly. When cool but still liquid, add to the cheese mixture with the chocolate. Mix well.

Whisk the egg whites until stiff and fold into the mixture. Pour over the biscuit base and chill in the refrigerator. When set, transfer to a serving plate and return to the refrigerator.

Dip the hazelnuts into the chocolate and leave to set on greaseproof paper. Decorate with cream and the hazelnuts.

Serves 6–8

---

far left: black forest gâteau
left: mocha cheesecake
right: orange truffle cake

Orange Truffle Cake

grated rind of 1 orange
1 quantity Genoese Sponge mixture
    (see page 48)
Filling:
150 ml (¼ pint) double or whipping
    cream
150 g (5 oz) plain chocolate, broken
    into pieces
1 tablespoon orange liqueur
    (optional)
Frosting:
50 g (2 oz) butter
50 g (2 oz) soft brown sugar
grated rind of 1 orange
2 tablespoons orange juice
250 g (8 oz) icing sugar, sifted
To decorate:
chocolate curls
icing sugar

Grease 2 x 20 cm (8 inch) sandwich tins. Fold the orange rind into the sponge mixture with the flour. Bake the sponge mixture in the sandwich tins in a preheated oven, 180°C (350°F), Gas Mark 4, for about 20 minutes until the sponges are well risen, golden brown and spring back when lightly pressed. Transfer to a wire rack to cool.

Meanwhile, make the filling. Bring the cream just to the boil. Away from the heat, stir in the chocolate and continue stirring until the mixture is smooth and thick. Stir in the liqueur, if using. Cool and chill for about 4 hours

until set. Spread the cooled truffle filling over one sponge and place the second sponge on top. Press down lightly.

To make the frosting, combine the butter, soft brown sugar, orange rind and juice in a pan. Heat gently, stirring, until the butter has melted and the sugar has dissolved, then boil for 1 minute.

Pour the mixture into the icing sugar and stir with a wooden spoon, gradually incorporating all the icing sugar. Beat well until smooth, then spoon over the cake and smooth with a palette knife. Decorate with chocolate curls and dust lightly with icing sugar.

Serves 8

Chocolate Cheesecake Flan

125 g (4 oz) Shortcrust Pastry (see
  page 54)
Filling:
250 g (8 oz) full-fat cream cheese
2 eggs, separated
25 g (1 oz) caster sugar
75 g (3 oz) plain chocolate, melted
1 tablespoon sherry
To decorate:
65 ml (2½ fl oz) double cream,
  whipped
white chocolate curls

Roll out the pastry and use to line a
20 cm (8 inch) fluted flan tin or
dish. Prick the base, line with
greaseproof paper and cover with
baking beans . Bake in a preheated
oven, 190°C (375°F), Gas Mark 5,
for 12 minutes. Remove the lining
and beans and cook for 5 minutes.

To make the filling, place the
cream cheese in a bowl and beat in
the egg yolks, sugar, chocolate and
sherry. In another bowl, whisk the
egg whites until stiff and fold into
the chocolate mixture. Spoon into
the flan case and return to the oven
for 25–30 minutes until the filling is
set. Allow to cool, then chill until
required.

Decorate with cream and white
chocolate curls.

Serves 6–8

Lemon Delight

3 eggs
75 g (3 oz) caster sugar
75 g (3 oz) plain flour, sifted
finely grated rind of ½ lemon
2 tablespoons lemon juice
2 tablespoons sherry
chocolate leaves, to decorate
Chocolate Fudge Frosting:
25 g (1 oz) butter or margarine
15 g (½ oz) soft brown sugar
2 teaspoons milk
25 g (1 oz) plain chocolate, broken
  into pieces
75 g (3 oz) icing sugar, sifted
Topping:
125 g (4 oz) skimmed milk soft
  cheese or curd cheese
grated rind of ½ lemon
2–3 tablespoons single cream
15 g (½ oz) icing sugar, sifted

Grease and base-line 2 x 18 cm
(7 inch) sandwich tins. In a large
bowl, whisk the eggs with the sugar
until the mixture is pale and thick
and the whisk leaves a trail. Fold in
the flour and lemon rind. Spoon the
mixture into the cake tins.

Bake in a preheated oven, 190°C
(375°F), Gas Mark 5, for 15–20
minutes until the cakes are firm and
springy. Invert on to a wire rack to
cool, then prick all over with a fork.
Mix together the lemon juice and
sherry and spoon over the cakes.

To make the fudge frosting, put
the butter or margarine, brown
sugar, milk and chocolate in a
saucepan and heat gently, stirring

occasionally, until smooth. Beat in the icing sugar.

Sandwich the cakes together with the chocolate fudge frosting and place on a serving plate.

To make the topping, put the cheese in a bowl and beat until softened. Add the lemon rind, single cream and icing sugar and mix well. Spread the mixture over the top of the cake and decorate with chocolate leaves.

Serves 6–8

left: lemon delight (top), chocolate cheesecake flan (bottom)
below: *chocolate loaf*

Chocolate Loaf

25 g (1 oz) bran
125 g (4 oz) sultanas
100 ml (3½ fl oz) orange juice
200 g (7 oz) self-raising flour
25 g (1 oz) cocoa powder
75 g (3 oz) block margarine
50 g (2 oz) soft brown sugar
50 g (2 oz) walnuts, chopped
½ teaspoon grated nutmeg
2 eggs
Filling and topping:
125 g (4 oz) curd cheese
75 g (3 oz) plain chocolate, melted
walnut halves
icing sugar, for dusting

Grease a 500 g (1 lb) loaf tin. Place the bran, sultanas and orange juice in a bowl; stand for 30 minutes.

Sift the flour and cocoa into a bowl and rub in the margarine until the mixture resembles breadcrumbs. Stir in the sugar, nuts, nutmeg, bran mixture and eggs to make a stiff dough. Spoon into the loaf tin and bake in a preheated oven, 160°C (325°F), Gas Mark 3, until well risen. Cool on a wire rack.

To make the filling, beat the cheese until smooth, then beat in the chocolate. Split the loaf into 2 layers, sandwich with half the filling and cover the top with the remainder. Decorate with walnut halves and dust with icing sugar.

Makes 10 slices

Mocha Strawberry Slice

8 sponge fingers

6 tablespoons cold, strong black coffee

250 g (8 oz) strawberries, sliced

150 ml (¼ pint) double cream

125 g (4 oz) skimmed milk soft cheese or curd cheese

40 g (1½ oz) soft brown sugar

125 g (4 oz) plain chocolate, melted

125 g (4 oz) digestive biscuits, crushed

2 tablespoons sherry

To decorate:

150 ml (¼ pint) double cream

2 teaspoons cold, strong, black coffee

Line a 500 g (1 lb) loaf tin with clingfilm so that it extends 2.5 cm (1 inch) above the rim. Arrange the sponge fingers, sugar-side down, on the base of the tin and pour over 5 tablespoons of the coffee. Arrange half the strawberry slices over the top. Combine the remaining coffee with the double cream in a bowl and whip until thick. Spread half the cream over the strawberry slices.

In another bowl, beat the cheese with the sugar until softened, then stir in the chocolate, biscuits and sherry. Mix well, then quickly spread half the quantity over the cream. Set aside 12 of the remaining strawberry slices and arrange the rest on top of the chocolate mixture. Spread the remaining coffee cream over the strawberry

slices and top with the remaining chocolate mixture.

Chill the loaf in the refrigerator until set, then turn out, carefully removing the clingfilm.

To decorate, whip the double cream and coffee until thick. Spread a thin layer over the top and sides. Pipe the rest on top and decorate with the reserved strawberry slices. Serve immediately.

Serves 6–8

Chocolate Mint Cheesecake

50 g (2 oz) margarine, melted

125 g (4 oz) digestive biscuits, crushed

40 g (1½) plain chocolate, melted

Filling:

375 g (12 oz) curd cheese

50 g (2 oz) caster sugar

200 ml (7 fl oz) single cream

½ teaspoon peppermint essence

3 tablespoons water

15 g (½ oz) powdered gelatine

50 g (2 oz) chocolate mint sticks, chopped

65 ml (2½ fl oz) whipping cream, whipped

To decorate:

whipped cream

mint sprigs

left: chocolate mint cheesecake (top), mocha strawberry slice (bottom)
right: spiced chocolate cheesecake

Mix together the margarine, biscuit crumbs and chocolate. Press on to the base of a 20 cm (8 inch) loose-bottomed cake tin. Leave in a cool place to set. Place the cheese and sugar in a bowl. Beat to soften slightly, then stir in the single cream and peppermint essence.

Pour the water into a small heatproof bowl and sprinkle the gelatine on top. Set aside for 2 minutes until spongy. Place the bowl over a saucepan of simmering water, stirring occasionally, until the gelatine has melted. Allow to cool slightly, then fold into the cheese mixture with the chocolate mint sticks and cream. Mix thoroughly, then spoon over the biscuit base. Chill until set. Transfer to a serving plate. Decorate with cream and mint sprigs.

Serves 8

Spiced Chocolate Cheesecake

125 g (4 oz) chocolate digestive
  biscuits, crushed
1 teaspoon mixed spice
50 g (2 oz) butter, melted
Filling:
2 eggs
50 g (2 oz) caster sugar
250 g (8 oz) skimmed milk soft
  cheese or curd cheese

25 g (1 oz) ground almonds
½ teaspoon grated nutmeg
75 g (3 oz) plain chocolate, melted
65 ml (2½ fl oz) double cream
To decorate:
65 ml (2½ fl oz) double cream,
  whipped
chocolate curls

Mix together the biscuit crumbs, mixed spice and melted butter. Press on to the base of a 20 cm (8 inch) loose-bottomed cake tin.

To make the filling, place the eggs and sugar in a bowl and whisk until thick and creamy. In a separate bowl, beat the cheese until

softened. Add the ground almonds, nutmeg, melted chocolate and cream and mix well. Gradually add the whisked egg mixture and stir together.

Spoon the filling over the biscuit base and bake in a preheated oven, 180°C (350°F), Gas Mark 4, for 40–50 minutes until firm. Allow the cheesecake to cool in the tin, then transfer to a serving plate and chill in the refrigerator.

Just before serving, decorate the cheesecake with whipped cream and chocolate curls.

Serves 6–8

Meringue Basket

4 egg whites

125 g (4 oz) caster sugar

125 g (4 oz) icing sugar

2 tablespoons cocoa powder, sifted

1 teaspoon vanilla essence

25 g (1 oz) chocolate vermicelli
  (optional)

250 g (8 oz) fresh raspberries

25 g (1 oz) plain chocolate, melted,
  to decorate

Filling:

200 g (7 oz) plain chocolate, broken
  into pieces

1 tablespoon milk

4 egg yolks

2 tablespoons liqueur, e.g. Cointreau,
  Tia Maria

450 ml (¾ pint) double or whipping
  cream, whipped

Draw 4 x 18 cm (7 inch) squares on 4 separate pieces of non-stick baking paper. Lay a piece of paper on each of 2 baking sheets.

Whisk the egg whites until standing in stiff peaks. Add all the caster sugar and continue beating until very stiff and standing in rigid peaks. Carefully fold in the icing sugar, cocoa and vanilla essence.

Spoon some of the meringue into a piping bag fitted with a 1 cm (½ inch) plain nozzle. Pipe straight lines to form a square on the non-stick baking paper on the baking sheets, using the drawn outlines as a guide. Spoon more meringue into the centre of each square and spread it with a spatula to form 2 solid squares of meringue. Spread the meringue up to the level of the piping.

Bake in a preheated oven, 110°C (225°F), Gas Mark ¼, for 1½–2 hours until completely dried out. Peel off the paper and cool.

Pipe the outline only of the squares on the 2 remaining sheets of paper. Bake and cool as before. Use up any remaining meringue mixture by piping ribbons of meringue around and inside the square outline to use as decoration.

To make the filling, melt the chocolate and milk in a heatproof bowl set over a pan of hot water. Stir until smooth. Away from the heat, add the egg yolks, 1 at a time, stirring well after each addition. Stir in the liqueur. Cool for about 2 hours until set.

About 1 hour before serving, spread 2 tablespoons of the cream over a solid base meringue and fit a square outline over the top. Spread a little more cream over the square outline and top with the remaining square outline.

Mask the sides of the meringue basket with cream and draw a serrated scraper across each side to form a ridged surface.

With a small palette knife, press on a narrow band of chocolate vermicelli, if using, about 1 cm (½ inch) from the bottom of the meringue basket.

Carefully transfer to a serving plate. Spoon the filling into the base. Reserve 12 raspberries for decoration and arrange the remainder on top of the filling.

Mask one side of the remaining solid square of meringue with a thin layer of cream and position over the basket, cream-side up. Spoon the remaining cream into a large piping bag fitted with a 3 mm (⅛ inch) plain nozzle. Pipe a series of parallel lines in one direction over the top of the basket.

Spoon the chocolate into a small greaseproof paper bag and snip the end to make a very small aperture. Drizzle the chocolate over the surface of the basket.

Decorate with the reserved raspberries and meringue ribbons.

Serves 8–10

Variation: Petits Vacherins
Using a half quantity of the meringue mixture above, spoon the mixture into a piping bag fitted with a 1 cm (½ inch) star nozzle. Pipe small nests no more than 3.5 cm (1½ inches) in diameter on to baking sheets lined with non-stick baking paper. Bake as above.

Using 250 ml (8 fl oz) double or whipping cream, whipped, pipe a swirl of cream into each vacherin. Top each with a small strawberry, quartered, mandarin orange segment, or grated chocolate.

right: kiwi choux

Kiwi Choux

65 g (2½ oz) plain flour
150 ml (¼ pint) cold water
50 g (2 oz) butter
2 eggs, beaten
Filling:
150 ml (¼ pint) double cream,
  whipped
125 g (4 oz) plain chocolate, melted
3 kiwi fruit, sliced
To decorate:
25 g (1 oz) plain chocolate, melted
icing sugar, sifted

Grease a baking sheet and mark a 20 cm (8 inch) circle. Make the choux pastry according to the instructions on page 19. Fill a large piping bag fitted with a plain nozzle with the choux pastry and pipe around the edge of the circle. Bake in a preheated oven, 200°C (400°F), Gas Mark 6, for 20 minutes. Make 2 slits in the sides of the choux to release the steam, then lower the temperature to 180°C (350°F), Gas Mark 4, and return to the oven for 10 minutes. Cool on a wire rack.

To make the filling, fold the cream and chocolate together until thoroughly mixed. Just before serving, cut the choux in half horizontally. Spread the chocolate cream over the base, then arrange the slices of kiwi on top. Cover with the remaining choux layer. Drizzle melted chocolate over and dust with icing sugar. Serve immediately.

Serves 4–6

Windmill Cake

This cake is best assembled when the Victoria sponge layers have been made 2–3 days in advance and stored in an airtight container.

½ quantity Chocolate Victoria sponge mixture (see page 56)
½ quantity Chocolate Victoria sponge mixture (see page 56), replacing the cocoa with flour
about 6 tablespoons seedless raspberry jelly, melted
250 g (8 oz) butter
500 g (1 lb) icing sugar, sifted
2 tablespoons peppermint essence
2 tablespoons cocoa powder
2 tablespoons boiling water
24 chocolate buttons or chocolate cut-out shapes, to decorate (optional)

Prepare and bake the two Victoria sponge mixtures in 20 cm (8 inch) round sandwich tins as directed on page 56. Cool on a wire rack.

Cut out 2 circular cardboard discs, 5 cm (2 inches) and 14 cm (5½ inches) in diameter, as templates.

Place the small template on one cake and cut round it. Place the large template on the same cake and cut round that. Carefully free the circles of cake. Repeat this process with the other cake.

Re-assemble the cake alternating the plain and chocolate circles. Brush each ring edge with a little warmed jelly to stick them together.

Cream the butter and half the icing sugar until light and fluffy. Beat in the remaining icing sugar. In separate bowls, divide the mixture into two-thirds and one-third portions.

Flavour the small portion by beating in the peppermint essence. Blend the cocoa with the water and leave to cool. Beat the cocoa into the large portion of buttercream.

Sandwich the cake layers together with one-third of the chocolate buttercream.

Divide the cake top and sides into 8 sections and pipe stars alternating the two types of buttercream. Finish the cake edges with the chocolate buttons or chocolate cut-out shapes, if using.

Makes 8–10 slices

Paris Brest Au Chocolat

1 quantity Choux Pastry (see page 19)
25 g (1 oz) flaked almonds
icing sugar, for dusting
Filling:
150 ml (¼ pint) milk
1 tablespoon instant custard powder
75 g (3 oz) plain chocolate, broken into pieces
250 ml (8 fl oz) double cream, whipped
1 quantity Praline (see page 91) (optional)

Grease a baking sheet. Spoon the choux pastry into a large piping bag fitted with a 1.5 cm (¾ inch) nozzle. Pipe a thick circle of pastry about 20 cm (8 inches) in diameter on the baking sheet.

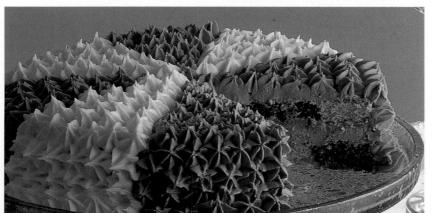

Sprinkle the choux pastry with the flaked almonds, then dust with icing sugar. Bake in a preheated oven, 200°C (400°F), Gas Mark 6, for 15 minutes, then reduce the heat to 190°C (375°F), Gas Mark 5, and bake for a further 15–20 minutes until the choux ring is well risen. Cover the choux ring loosely with foil if the flaked almonds brown too quickly.

Split the cooked ring open to release the steam and return to the oven for 5 minutes to dry out. Cool on a wire rack.

To make the filling, blend the milk and custard powder, pour into a pan and bring to the boil, stirring constantly. Cool slightly, then cover closely with clingfilm or damp greaseproof paper to prevent a skin forming. Leave until cold.

Place the chocolate in a small heatproof bowl and set over a pan of simmering water to melt.

Stir the melted chocolate into the custard. When smooth, fold in the cream, and praline, if using. Place the base of the choux ring on a serving dish and spoon on the chocolate filling. Replace the top and dust with icing sugar. Eat on the same day.

Serves 4–6

left: paris brest au chocolat (top), windmill cake (bottom)
right: chocolate basket

Chocolate Basket

This impressive gateau is ideal for special occasions. For a simpler version, spread the buttercream over the cake using a palette knife.

1 quantity Chocolate Victoria sponge mixture (see page 56)
2 quantities Chocolate Buttercream Icing (see page 56)
about 24 chocolate leaves
about 12 glacé cherries, some halved and some quartered
icing sugar, for dusting (optional)

Bake the chocolate Victoria sponge mixture in 2 x 20 cm (8 inch) sandwich tins in a preheated oven, 180°C (350°F), Gas Mark 4, for 25–30 minutes. Remove the sponges from the tins and transfer to a wire rack to cool.

Cut each cake into 2 layers. Sandwich 3 layers together, using 3 tablespoons of the buttercream for each layer, ending with a layer of buttercream.

Using a small tea plate as a guide, cut a disc about 15 cm (6 inches) in diameter out of the remaining cake layer. Coat the top with a thin layer of buttercream and place the outer ring on the top of the cake.

Fit a piping bag with a ribbon nozzle and fill with the remaining buttercream. Pipe a basketwork design on the side of the cake and on the top and side of the 15 cm (6 inch) layer of cake.

Arrange the chocolate leaves over the rim around the cake. Position the glacé cherries at intervals.

Carefully lower the small layer of cake on top of the leaves and glacé cherries and lightly dust with icing sugar, if liked.

Serves 6–8

Chocolate Apricot Cheesecake

50 g (2 oz) butter, melted

125 g (4 oz) digestive biscuits, crushed

Filling:

1 x 425 g (14 oz) can apricots in fruit juice, drained

250 g (8 oz) skimmed milk soft cheese or curd cheese

50 g (2 oz) caster sugar

150 g (5 oz) Greek yogurt

2 eggs, separated

125 g (4 oz) plain chocolate, melted

Topping:

150 ml (¼ pint) soured cream

chocolate curls

Grease a loose-bottomed 20 cm (8 inch) cake tin. Mix the butter with the biscuit crumbs in a bowl. Press on to the base of the cake tin. Leave in a cool place to set.

Spoon the apricots over the base. In a large bowl, beat the cheese with the sugar until softened, then stir in the yogurt and egg yolks. Mix well, then stir in the chocolate.

Whisk the egg whites until stiff and fold into the mixture. Spoon over the apricots and bake in a preheated oven, 180°C (350°F), Gas Mark 4, for 45 minutes–1 hour until set.

Place the soured cream in a bowl and beat until smooth. Spread over the cheesecake. Reduce the oven temperature to 150°C (300°F), Gas Mark 2, and return the cheesecake to the oven for 15 minutes.

Leave the cheesecake to cool in the tin, then transfer to a serving plate. Chill until required. Decorate with chocolate curls and serve.

Serves 6–8

Cranberry Gâteau

4 eggs, separated

150 g (5 oz) icing sugar, sifted

65 g (2½ oz) plain flour

15 g (½ oz) cornflour

25 g (1 oz) cocoa powder

½ teaspoon baking powder

3 drops vanilla essence

1 tablespoon milk

Filling:

75 g (3 oz) cranberry sauce

150 ml (¼ pint) double cream,
  whipped

Topping:

150 ml (¼ pint) soured cream

150 g (5 oz) white chocolate, melted

2 tablespoons skimmed milk soft
  cheese or curd cheese, softened

To decorate:

chocolate leaves

chocolate curls

Mix the egg yolks and icing sugar in a large bowl and whisk until pale and fluffy. In a separate bowl, whisk the egg whites until stiff and fold into the egg yolk mixture.

Sift together the plain flour, cornflour, cocoa powder and baking powder. Fold into the mixture with the vanilla essence and milk. Grease and base-line 3 x 18 cm (7 inch) sandwich tins and divide the mixture between them. Bake in a preheated oven, 180°C (350°F), Gas Mark 4, for 12–15 minutes. Cool the cakes in the tins for 5 minutes, then invert on to wire racks to cool.

To make the filling, stir the cranberry sauce gently into the double cream and use to sandwich the 3 cake layers together.

To make the topping, stir the soured cream into the melted white chocolate. Gradually add the softened cheese. Spread the mixture over the top and side of the cake.

Transfer the gateau to a serving plate and decorate with chocolate leaves and chocolate curls. Store the cranberry gateau in the refrigerator until required.

Serves 8

Coconut Chocolate Cheesecake

50 g (2 oz) butter

50 g (2 oz) caster sugar

40 g (1½ oz) plain flour

75 g (3 oz) desiccated coconut

Filling:

2 eggs, separated

50 g (2 oz) soft brown sugar

2 tablespoons cornflour

3 teaspoons cocoa powder

200 ml (7 fl oz) milk

250 g (8 oz) skimmed milk soft
  cheese or curd cheese

150 ml (¼ pint) double cream,
  whipped

Topping:

grated chocolate

desiccated coconut

Grease a 23 cm (9 inch) flan dish. In a mixing bowl, cream the butter with the sugar until light and fluffy, then mix in the flour and coconut. Press the mixture on to the base and side of the flan dish. Chill for 30 minutes, then bake in a preheated oven, 180°C (350°F), Gas Mark 4, for 15–20 minutes until golden brown. Allow to cool.

Place the egg yolks in a large bowl. Add the brown sugar, cornflour and cocoa powder and mix well. Heat the milk in a saucepan until just boiling, then stir into the egg yolk mixture. Return to the saucepan and cook, stirring, until the mixture thickens. Cover the surface of the custard with clingfilm or damp greaseproof and leave to cool.

Beat the cheese in a large bowl with a little of the cooled custard, then add the remaining custard. Mix well, and fold in half the double cream, reserving the remainder for decoration.

In a separate bowl, whisk the egg whites until stiff. Fold into the cheese mixture, then spoon on to the coconut base in the flan dish. Chill until required. Just before serving, decorate with the reserved whipped cream, the grated chocolate and coconut.

Serves 6–8

left: coconut chocolate cheesecake (far left), cranberry gâteau (top), chocolate apricot cheesecake (bottom)

Ganache Torte

4 eggs, separated
125 g (4 oz) caster sugar, plus
  1 tablespoon
50 g (2 oz) plain flour
50 g (2 oz) cornflour
50 g (2 oz) granulated sugar
50 ml (2 fl oz) water
3 tablespoons rum
150 ml (¼ pint) double or whipping
  cream, whipped
Crème Ganache:
150 ml (¼ pint) double cream
300 g (10 oz) plain chocolate, melted
To decorate:
12 small chocolate wedges
chocolate curls

Grease 2 x 20 cm (8 inch) deep sandwich tins. Place the egg yolks and the 125 g (4 oz) of sugar in a large bowl set over a pan of hot, not boiling, water. Whisk until the mixture becomes light, foamy and creamy.

Sift the flour and cornflour together. Whisk the egg whites and the tablespoon caster sugar until standing in soft peaks, then fold into the egg yolk mixture with the flour. Using a large metal spoon, make a figure-of-eight cutting action to fold the mixture lightly but thoroughly until evenly blended.

Divide the mixture between the sandwich tins. Smooth level with a spatula, then bake in a preheated oven, 160°C (325°F), Gas Mark 3, for about 20 minutes until well risen and golden brown. Turn out and cool on a wire rack. Slice each sandwich into 2 layers.

Dissolve the granulated sugar in the water over a gentle heat, then bring to the boil. Away from the heat, stir in the rum, then spoon the mixture over the cake layers.

To make the crème ganache, heat the cream in a saucepan, then gradually beat into the chocolate. Leave to cool, then beat again.

Beat half the cream into the crème ganache. Use one-third of the mixture to sandwich the layers of cake together. Press down well.

Use the remaining mixture to cover the entire gâteau, spreading it evenly. If liked, use a serrated comb or knife to ridge the sides of the cake. When set, mark the top of the gâteau into 12 sections with a sharp knife. Pipe a small rosette with the remaining cream in each section and 1 in the centre.

Press a chocolate wedge into each rosette and sprinkle chocolate curls over the centre rosette. The torte is best eaten the same day.

Makes 12 slices

Mocha Cheesecake

175 g (6 oz) butter
175 g (6 oz) digestive biscuits,
  crushed
75 g (3 oz) caster sugar
2 eggs, separated
5 teaspoons instant coffee powder or
  granules
2 tablespoons boiling water
½ teaspoon vanilla essence
4 tablespoons single cream or top of
  the milk
1 tablespoon cornflour
500 g (1 lb) curd cheese
125 g (4 oz) plain chocolate, coarsely
  chopped
To decorate:
icing sugar
25 g (1 oz) plain chocolate, finely
  grated

Melt 50 g (2 oz) of the butter in a pan, stir in the biscuit crumbs and mix thoroughly. Press the mixture on to the base of a 23 cm (9 inch) loose-bottomed cake tin.

Cream the butter and sugar until light and fluffy, then beat in the egg yolks 1 at a time.

Blend the coffee with the water and add to the mixture with the vanilla essence, cream or top of the milk and cornflour. Mix well then beat in the curd cheese and chocolate.

Whisk the egg whites until standing in soft peaks and carefully fold into the mixture.

Pour over the biscuit base and smooth level with a spatula. Bake in a preheated oven, 160°C (325°F), Gas Mark 3, for 1 hour until set. Turn off the oven and leave the cheesecake in the oven to cool. (The cheesecake will rise slightly during cooking, but will fall on cooling.)

To decorate, place a 10 cm

(4 inch) diameter disc of paper or card in the centre of the cheesecake and dust the cake with icing sugar. Carefully remove the disc and spoon the finely grated chocolate into the centre.

Serves 8

Chocolate Savarin

To obtain neat orange slices without any pith on them, cut a slice off the top and bottom of each orange and stand it on a board. With a small serrated knife, make smooth downward cuts following the curve of the orange. When you have been round the orange once, repeat the process to make sure all the pith has been removed.

140 g (4½ oz) strong plain flour
20 g (¾ oz) fresh yeast or 2 teaspoons dried yeast
15 g (½ oz) caster sugar
4 tablespoons milk, warmed to blood heat
2 eggs, beaten
45 g (1¾ oz) butter
Syrup:
125 g (4 oz) granulated sugar
1 tablespoon instant coffee
1 tablespoon cocoa powder
2 tablespoons brandy or cognac
To decorate:
4 oranges, peeled and sliced
julienne strips of orange rind

Butter a 1.2 litre (2 pint) savarin or ring mould. Sift the flour into a warm bowl.

Cream the fresh yeast with 1 teaspoon of the sugar and gradually add the warm milk, then the eggs. If using dried yeast, sprinkle the yeast over the warmed milk and add 1 teaspoon of the sugar. Leave in a warm place covered with a cloth for 15 minutes until frothy, then beat in the eggs.

Tip the liquid into the flour and beat with a wooden spoon for 5 minutes, or 1 minute with an electric mixer. Cover the bowl with a damp cloth and leave it in a warm place for about 40 minutes until the mixture doubles in bulk.

Cream the butter with the remaining sugar until soft and light, then beat into the risen mixture for 5 minutes with a wooden spoon, or 1 minute with an electric mixer.

Pour the batter into the tin and put in a warm place until it has risen to the top of the tin. Bake in a preheated oven, 200°C (400°F), Gas Mark 6, for 20–30 minutes until the savarin is browned and springs back when pressed lightly.

Meanwhile, make the syrup. Heat the sugar and 150 ml (¼ pint) water in a heavy-based pan until the sugar dissolves. Simmer for 5 minutes.

Blend the coffee and cocoa with 2 tablespoons hot water and stir into the warm syrup. Add the brandy or cognac.

Loosen the savarin from the tin. While it is still warm, pierce a few holes with a fine skewer and spoon over the syrup until the savarin is thoroughly soaked.

Carefully turn the savarin out on to a serving dish and leave to cool. Arrange the orange slices overlapping in the centre of the savarin and decorate with the julienne strips of orange rind.

Serves 4

above: mocha cheesecake (left), chocolate savarin (right)

Chocolate Meringue Torte

36 sponge fingers, crumbled

grated rind of 2 oranges

150 ml (¼ pint) orange juice

75 g (3 oz) sunflower margarine

75 g (3 oz) caster sugar

15 g (½ oz) cocoa powder

1 egg yolk

25 g (1 oz) walnuts, chopped

50 g (2 oz) plain chocolate, melted

1 tablespoon sherry

150 ml (¼ pint) whipping cream,
  whipped

Meringues:

1 egg white

50 g (2 oz) caster sugar

Line an 18 cm (7 inch) loose-bottomed cake tin with foil. Line a baking sheet with baking paper. Put the sponge finger crumbs into a bowl and add the orange rind and juice. Mix well and set aside until all the juice has been absorbed.

In another bowl, cream the margarine with the sugar until pale and fluffy. Stir in the cocoa powder, egg yolk, walnuts, chocolate and sherry. Mix thoroughly. Press half the sponge finger mixture into the cake tin. Spread the chocolate mixture over the top, then add the remaining sponge finger mixture. Cover and refrigerate until set.

In a large bowl, whisk the egg white until stiff, then whisk in the sugar 1 tablespoonful at a time. Using a piping bag fitted with a large star nozzle, pipe 8–10 small meringue rosettes on the baking sheet. Bake in a preheated oven, 120°C (250°F), Gas Mark ½, for 1 hour. Turn off the oven, leaving the meringues inside to cool gradually for several hours.

Turn out the chocolate torte and remove the foil. Cover with cream, then arrange the meringues on top. Serve within 1 hour.

Serves 8–10

*above: chocolate meringue torte
(top), chocolate walnut gâteau
(bottom)*
***right:** blackcurrant ring*

Chocolate Walnut Gâteau

3 eggs
75 g (3 oz) caster sugar
50 g (2 oz) plain flour
25 g (1 oz) cocoa powder
Filling and topping:
150 ml (¼ pint) whipping cream, whipped
50 g (2 oz) walnuts, chopped finely
½ quantity Chocolate Buttercream Icing (see page 56)
1 teaspoon instant coffee granules
To decorate:
3 large chocolate flake bars
walnut halves

Grease and base-line a 30 x 20 cm (12 x 8 inch) Swiss roll tin. In a large bowl, whisk the eggs with the sugar until the mixture is pale and thick and the whisk leaves a trail. Sift the flour and cocoa powder together and fold into the egg mixture. Pour into the tin.

Bake in a preheated oven, 200°C (400°F), Gas Mark 6, for 10-12 minutes until firm. Carefully invert the cake on to a wire rack to cool. Peel off the paper and cut the cake widthways into 3 equal pieces.

To make the filling, mix the cream with the walnuts and use to sandwich the 3 cake layers together. Prepare the chocolate buttercream icing, first mixing the coffee granules with the cocoa powder and boiling water listed in the buttercream recipe. Spread the buttercream over the gâteau top and sides.

Cut each chocolate flake into 3 equal lengths, then shave into small pieces and press to the side of the gâteau. Use the crumbled pieces that remain and the walnut halves to decorate the top.

Serves 8–10

Blackcurrant Ring

30 g (1¼ oz) butter, melted
4 eggs
125 g (4 oz) caster sugar
75 g (3 oz) plain flour
25 g (1 oz) cocoa powder
Filling:
250 g (8 oz) blackcurrants
50 g (2 oz) granulated or caster sugar
150 ml (¼ pint) double cream, whipped
2 tablespoons blackcurrant yogurt

Brush a 1.2 litre (2 pint) ring mould with a little of the melted butter.

Whisk the eggs and sugar until pale and thick. Sift the flour and cocoa powder together and fold half into the egg mixture. Stir in the butter, then fold in the remaining flour mixture. Pour into the ring mould and bake in a preheated oven, 180°C (350°F), Gas Mark 4, for 15–20 minutes until well risen.

Turn out on a wire rack to cool. Mix the blackcurrants, sugar and 1 tablespoon water in a pan and heat gently until the fruit is soft. Allow to cool. Spoon a little cream into a piping bag fitted with a star nozzle and set aside. Mix the remaining cream with the blackcurrants and yogurt. Cut the cake in half horizontally and sandwich together with the blackcurrant cream. Decorate with the reserved cream.

Serves 6

Valentine Gâteau

25 g (1 oz) hazelnuts, finely ground

1 quantity Genoese Sponge mixture
   (see right)

300 ml (½ pint) whipping cream,
   whipped

50 g (2 oz) plain chocolate, grated

250 g (8 oz) firm strawberries

½ quantity hot Crème Ganache (see
   page 44)

chocolate leaves, to decorate

icing sugar, for dusting (optional)

Grease and flour 2 x 18 cm (7 inch) heart-shaped tins, measured at the widest part.

Fold the hazelnuts into the sponge mixture with the flour. Divide the mixture between the tins and bake in a preheated oven, 180°C (350°F), Gas Mark 4, for 15–20 minutes until well risen and golden brown and the sponge springs back when lightly pressed.

Turn out on to a wire rack to cool.

Split each heart into 2 layers. Fold the cream and grated chocolate together and spread one-third over one sponge.

Reserve 3 strawberries with stalks for decoration, then slice some of the remaining even-sized strawberries to obtain 24 thin slices. Roughly chop the remainder.

Spread the chopped strawberries over the first layer of cream then smooth over a little more cream and place a second sponge on top. Halve the remaining cream and sandwich the remaining sponges with the cream.

Stand the gâteau on a wire rack and pour over the crème ganache. Smooth over quickly with a small palette knife. Leave to set for about 15 minutes.

Arrange the sliced strawberries in a row around the base of the gâteau. Place the 3 whole strawberries in a cluster on top of the gâteau and surround with chocolate leaves.

Leave to set for about 2 hours. If liked, sprinkle over a fine layer of icing sugar just before serving. Once assembled, this gâteau is best eaten on the day that it is made.

Serves 8

Genoese Sponge

4 eggs

125 g (4 oz) caster sugar

125 g (4 oz) plain flour, plus extra for
   dusting

25 g (1 oz) butter, melted, plus extra
   for brushing

Brush 2 x 20 cm (8 inch) deep-sided sandwich tins with melted butter and dust with flour.

Whisk the eggs and sugar until the mixture becomes very thick and light.

Sift half the flour over the surface of the mixture. Add half the melted butter. With a metal spoon, fold in the flour uusing a cutting figure-of-eight action until all the flour has been incorporated. Repeat with the remaining flour and butter. Fold as lightly and as little as possible.

Pour the mixture into the prepared tins and tilt until the mixture is evenly spread in the tins.

Bake in a preheated oven, 180°C (350°F), Gas Mark 4, for 15–20 minutes until the sponge is well risen and golden brown, and springs back when lightly pressed with a finger. Turn out and set aside to cool on a wire rack.

Chocolate Meringue Layer

140 g (4½ oz) icing sugar

2 egg whites

1 teaspoon vanilla essence

Filling:

125 g (4 oz) almonds, finely chopped
    and toasted

½ quantity hot Crème Ganache (see
    page 44)

1 teaspoon instant coffee powder or
    granules

1 tablespoon boiling water

2 tablespoons orange liqueur, rum or
    brandy

150 ml (¼ pint) double or whipping
    cream, whipped

To decorate:

50 ml (2 fl oz) double or whipping
    cream, whipped

chocolate curls

Draw an 18 cm (7 inch) diameter circle on 3 separate sheets of non-stick baking paper. Place on 2 baking sheets.

Put the icing sugar, egg whites and vanilla essence into a large bowl set over a saucepan of hot water. Whisk until the mixture becomes thick and glossy and stands in stiff peaks. Remove from the heat and beat until cool.

Divide the mixture into 3 portions. Spoon into the circles drawn on the paper and spread evenly with a spatula. Bake in 2 batches in a preheated oven, 150°C (300°F), Gas Mark 2, for about 1½–2 hours until crisp and thoroughly dried out. Carefully remove the non-stick baking paper and transfer the meringues on to wire racks to cool.

To make the filling, beat the almonds into the crème ganache. Blend the coffee with the boiling water and beat into the chocolate mixture with the alcohol. Chill for 4 hours.

Beat the filling well, then fold in the cream. Divide into 2 portions and use to sandwich the meringue layers together.

To decorate, spread the cream on top of the gâteau and decorate with the chocolate curls.

Serves 6–8

left: valentine gâteau
***above:** chocolate meringue layer*

Family Cakes

Chocolate Chip Scones

250 g (8 oz) self-raising flour
1 teaspoon baking powder
50 g (2 oz) margarine
6 tablespoons milk
2 tablespoons chocolate yogurt
50 g (2 oz) plain chocolate drops
milk, for brushing

Grease a baking sheet. Sift the flour and baking powder into a bowl, add the margarine and rub in until the mixture resembles fine breadcrumbs. Add the milk, yogurt and chocolate drops, then mix to a stiff dough.

Turn the dough on to a floured surface and knead lightly until smooth. Roll out to a round 1.5 cm (¾ inch) thick, then, using a 6 cm (2½ inch) fluted cutter, cut 8–10 scones. Place on the baking sheet, allowing room for expansion, then brush with milk. Bake in a preheated oven, 220°C (425°F), Gas Mark 7, for 12–15 minutes until well risen and browned.

Transfer the scones to a wire rack to cool slightly. Serve warm.

Makes 8–10

Chequered Chocolate Cake

This attractive cake becomes more moist if kept in an airtight tin for 1–3 days after decorating but before cutting.

125 g (4 oz) plain flour
125 g (4 oz) wholemeal flour
25 g (1 oz) cocoa powder
150 g (5 oz) caster sugar
1½ teaspoons bicarbonate of soda
1½ teaspoons baking powder
pinch of salt
125 g (4 oz) sunflower margarine
200 ml (7 fl oz) milk
3 eggs
1½ tablespoons black treacle
Vanilla Buttercream Icing:
75 g (3 oz) butter, softened
175 g (6 oz) icing sugar, sifted
few drops vanilla essence
To decorate:
¾ quantity Chocolate Buttercream
  Icing (see page 56)
chocolate triangles

Grease and base-line a 23 cm (9 inch) square cake tin. Sift the dry ingredients into a bowl and mix well. Make a well in the centre and add the remaining ingredients. Beat well for 2–3 minutes. Spoon into the tin. Bake in a preheated oven, 160°C (325°F), Gas Mark 3, for

40–45 minutes until firm and a skewer inserted in the centre comes out clean. Invert on to a wire rack to cool.

Cut the cake in half horizontally.

To make the vanilla buttercream, beat the margarine until creamy. Gradually add the icing sugar, beating well. Beat in vanilla essence to taste. Spread a thin layer of the buttercream over the base of the cake. Cover with the top half of the cake and spread a thin layer of chocolate buttercream over the cake. Mark the top into 7 cm (3 inch) squares. Place the remaining chocolate and vanilla buttercreams in 2 separate piping bags fitted with small star nozzles.

Use the chocolate buttercream to fill in the 4 outer corners and the centre square with small stars. Using the vanilla buttercream, fill in the remaining squares in the same way. Stand the chocolate triangles between the squares so that the points are uppermost.

Makes 18 slices

right: chequered chocolate cake, chocolate chip scones, orange chocolate teabread

Orange Chocolate Teabread

300 g (10 oz) mixed dried fruit
50 g (2 oz) soft brown sugar
300 ml (½ pint) orange juice

1 egg, beaten
300 g (10 oz) self-raising flour
25 g (1 oz) drinking chocolate
   powder

Grease a 1 kg (2 lb) loaf tin. Place the dried fruit, sugar and orange juice in a large bowl. Cover and leave to soak for 4–5 hours.

Add the egg, flour and drinking chocolate and mix well. Spoon the mixture into the loaf tin. Bake in a preheated oven, 180°C (350°F), Gas Mark 4, for 45 minutes–1 hour until a skewer inserted in the centre comes out clean. Leave to cool on a wire rack. Serve sliced and spread with butter.

Makes 18–20 slices

Mocha Swiss Roll

1 tablespoon instant coffee granules

1 tablespoon hot water

3 eggs

75 g (3 oz) caster sugar

65 g (2½ oz) plain flour

15 g (½ oz) cocoa powder

caster sugar, for dredging

½ quantity Chocolate Buttercream
   Icing (see page 56)

Grease and line a 30 x 20 cm (12 x 8 inch) Swiss roll tin. Mix the coffee granules with the hot water until dissolved, then leave to cool.

Place the eggs and sugar in a bowl and whisk with an electric mixer or a rotary whisk until the mixture is pale and thick and the whisk leaves a trail. Sift the flour and cocoa powder into the mixture and fold in lightly with the cooled coffee. Pour into the tin and tilt until evenly distributed and level. Bake in a preheated oven, 200°C (400°F), Gas Mark 6, for 10–12 minutes.

Lay a piece of greaseproof paper on a damp tea towel and sprinkle with caster sugar. Invert the cake on to the paper; peel away the lining paper. Trim the edges and roll up with the help of the tea towel. Transfer to a wire rack to cool. Gently unroll the cake and spread with buttercream. Roll up again and sprinkle with extra caster sugar.

Makes 8–10 slices

Chocolate Chestnut Eclairs

1 quantity Choux Pastry (see page 19)

½ x 439 g (15½ oz) can unsweetened
   chestnut purée

150 g (5 oz) natural fromage frais

50 g (2 oz) icing sugar, sifted

50 g (2 oz) plain chocolate, melted

Grease a baking sheet. Spoon the choux pastry into a piping bag fitted with a 1.5 cm (¾ inch) plain nozzle. Pipe 8 x 8 cm (3½ inch) fingers, at least 7 cm (3 inches) apart on the baking sheet. Bake in a preheated oven, 200°C (400°F), Gas Mark 6, for 15 minutes, then reduce the temperature to 180°C (350°F), Gas Mark 4, and bake for 10 minutes more.

Place the eclairs on a wire rack, slitting the sides to allow steam to escape. Leave to cool.

In a bowl, combine the chestnut purée, fromage frais and icing sugar. Mix well. Just before serving, split the eclairs and fill with the chestnut mixture. Spread the tops with melted chocolate.

Makes 8

Marbled Meringues

2 egg whites
125 g (4 oz) caster sugar
50 g (2 oz) plain chocolate, finely
  grated
150 ml (¼ pint) double cream,
  whipped
2 small chocolate flake bars, crumbled

Line a baking sheet with baking
paper. Whisk the egg whites until
stiff, then add the sugar,
1 tablespoonful at a time, whisking
well. Fold in the grated chocolate.

Spoon the meringue mixture into
a large piping bag fitted with a
1.5 cm (¾ inch) plain or fluted
nozzle and pipe 12 small oblong
shapes of equal size on to the paper,
allowing room for expansion. Bake
in a preheated oven, 120°C (250°F),
Gas Mark ½ for 1 hour. Turn off the
oven, leaving the meringues inside
to cool gradually for about 8 hours
or overnight.

Fold the cream and chocolate
flakes together. Use to sandwich the
meringues in pairs. Serve the
meringues immediately.

Makes 6

*left: chocolate chestnut eclairs, mocha
swiss roll*
right: *marbled meringues*

Chocolate-coated Tarts

75 g (3 oz) dried apricots
2 tablespoons water
12 teaspoons ginger preserve
Shortcrust Pastry:
125 g (4 oz) plain flour
pinch of salt
25 g (1 oz) margarine
25 g (1 oz) lard or white vegetable fat
1 tablespoon water
Topping:
75 g (3 oz) plain chocolate, melted

Place the apricots and water in a bowl and leave to soak for 2 hours.

Sift the flour and salt into a bowl, add the margarine and lard or white vegetable fat and rub in until the mixture resembles fine breadcrumbs. Add the water and mix to a stiff dough, then turn on to a floured board and knead until smooth. Roll out, then, using a 7 cm (3 inch) fluted cutter, cut rounds to line 12 tartlet tins.

Drain the apricots, chop them finely and divide among the pastry cases. Top each with 1 teaspoon ginger preserve extra jam. Bake in a preheated oven, 190°C (375°F), Gas Mark 5, for 15 minutes. Cool in the tin for 5 minutes, then transfer to a wire rack to cool.

Spread melted chocolate over the preserve and allow to set.

Makes 12

Chocolate Streusel Cake

125 g (4 oz) self-raising flour
1 teaspoon baking powder
125 g (4 oz) sunflower margarine
2 eggs
Topping:
50 g (2 oz) plain flour
2 teaspoons cocoa powder
25 g (1 oz) butter
50 g (2 oz) demerara sugar
25 g (1 oz) white chocolate, grated, to decorate

Grease and base-line an 18 cm (7 inch) square cake tin. Place all the cake ingredients in a bowl and beat together to make a smooth batter. Spoon into the cake tin.

To make the topping, sift the flour and cocoa powder into a bowl, add the butter and rub in until the mixture resembles fine breadcrumbs. Stir in the sugar and spoon the mixture over the cake batter.

Bake in a preheated oven, 180°C (350°F), Gas Mark 4, for 30–40 minutes until firm and a skewer inserted into the centre comes out clean. Leave in the tin for 5 minutes, then transfer to a wire rack to cool completely. Decorate with grated white chocolate.

Makes 10–12 slices

Chocolate Rock Buns

200 g (7 oz) self-raising flour
25 g (1 oz) cocoa powder
75 g (3 oz) caster sugar
75 g (3 oz) margarine
2 eggs, beaten
2 tablespoons milk
75 g (3 oz) plain or milk chocolate drops

Grease 2 baking sheets. Sift the flour and cocoa powder into a bowl and stir in the sugar. Add the margarine and rub in until the mixture resembles fine breadcrumbs. Add the eggs and milk, then mix to a stiff dough. Stir in the chocolate drops.

Place spoonfuls of the mixture on to the baking sheets, allowing space for expansion. Bake in a preheated oven, 200°C (400°F), Gas Mark 6, for 15–20 minutes. Transfer to a wire rack to cool.

Makes 15–16

left: chocolate rock buns, chocolate-coated tarts, chocolate streusel cake
above: wholemeal chocolate fudge cake

Wholemeal Chocolate Fudge Cake

25 g (1 oz) cocoa powder

1 tablespoon instant coffee granules

125 ml (4 fl oz) hot water

125 g (4 oz) sunflower margarine

125 g (4 oz) soft brown sugar

3 eggs, beaten

75 g (3 oz) plain chocolate, melted

250 g (8 oz) self-raising wholemeal flour

Frosting:

250 g (8 oz) carton skimmed milk soft cheese or curd cheese

75 g (3 oz) plain chocolate, melted

To decorate:

grated chocolate

chocolate caraque

Grease and base-line a 20 cm (8 inch) cake tin. Mix the cocoa powder and coffee granules with the hot water. Cream the margarine and sugar until light and fluffy, then gradually add the eggs, beating well after each addition. Stir in the coffee mixture and the chocolate, then fold in the flour and mix well.

Spoon into the cake tin and bake in a preheated oven, 180°C (350°F), Gas Mark 4, for 30–40 minutes until firm. Invert on to a wire rack to cool. Cut in half horizontally.

Beat the cheese until softened. Beat in the chocolate. Use half to sandwich the cake layers together. Spread the rest smoothly over the top. Decorate with bands of grated chocolate and caraque. Cover and refrigerate until required.

Makes 8–10 slices

Marble Cake

125 g (4 oz) sunflower margarine
125 g (4 oz) caster sugar
2 eggs, beaten
125 g (4 oz) self-raising flour, sifted
2 teaspoons cold milk
pink food colouring
green food colouring
2 teaspoons cocoa powder
2 drops vanilla essence
To decorate:
1½ teaspoons cocoa powder
2 teaspoons boiling water
½ quantity Glacé Icing (see page 59)
chocolate-flavoured sugar strands

Grease a fluted 18 cm (7 inch) cake tin. Place the margarine, sugar, eggs, flour and milk in a bowl and beat together for 2–3 minutes. Divide among 3 bowls. Tint one portion with pink colouring and another with green colouring. Stir the cocoa powder and vanilla essence into the remaining bowl. Mix the contents of each bowl well. Place alternate spoonfuls of each mixture in the cake tin. Level the top.

Bake in a preheated oven, 180°C (350°F), Gas Mark 4, for 30–35 minutes until a skewer inserted into the centre comes out clean. Invert on to a wire rack to cool.

Dissolve the cocoa powder in the boiling water and gradually add with the icing sugar when making the glacé icing. Pipe over the cake. Sprinkle the sugar strands on top.

Makes 8–10 slices

Chocolate Victoria Sponge

250 g (8 oz) butter, softened
250 g (8 oz) caster sugar
4 eggs, beaten
200 g (7 oz) self-raising flour
50 g (2 oz) cocoa powder
1 tablespoon milk
3 drops vanilla essence
chocolate buttons, to decorate
Chocolate Buttercream Icing:
2 tablespoons cocoa powder
2 tablespoons boiling water
125 g (4 oz) butter, softened
250 g (8 oz) icing sugar, sifted

Grease and base-line 2 x 20 cm (8 inch) deep-sided sandwich tins. Cream the butter and sugar together until pale and fluffy. Add the eggs, a little at a time, beating well.

Sift the flour and cocoa powder together. Fold half the mixture into the bowl, add the milk, then fold in the remaining flour with the vanilla essence. Mix well. Divide the cake mixture between the tins. Bake in a preheated oven, 180°C (350°F), Gas Mark 4, for 25–30 minutes until risen and a skewer inserted into the centre comes out clean. Leave in the tins for 5 minutes, then invert the cakes on to a wire rack to cool.

Blend the cocoa powder with the water. Cream the butter and half the sugar until light and fluffy. Gradually work in the remaining icing sugar, then beat in the cocoa paste.

Sandwich the cakes together with half the buttercream. Use most of the remainder to cover the top of the cake, reserving some to pipe rosettes around the edge. Decorate with chocolate button halves.

Makes 8–10 slices

Bran Muffins

125 g (4 oz) wholemeal flour
75 g (3 oz) high-fibre bran cereal, crushed
2 teaspoons baking powder
1 tablespoon cocoa powder
1 tablespoon drinking chocolate powder
25 g (1 oz) soft brown sugar
1 egg
4 tablespoons sunflower oil
250 ml (8 fl oz) milk

Grease 12 deep bun tins or 18 shallow tartlet tins. Combine the first 6 ingredients. Mix thoroughly, then make a well in the centre.

Whisk the egg and oil together and add the milk. Pour into the well and gradually incorporate with the dry ingredients. Beat well. Spoon into the tins. Bake in a preheated oven, 200°C (400°F), Gas Mark 6, for 25–35 minutes until risen and firm. Serve warm, with butter.

Makes 12–18

right: marble cake, chocolate victoria sponge, bran muffins

Chocolate, Carrot and Raisin Cake

This cake improves with keeping, so make it a day or two before serving and store in an airtight tin; the carrots help keep it moist.

150 g (5 oz) soft brown sugar
125 g (4 oz) margarine
175 g (6 oz) carrots, grated
125 g (4 oz) raisins
250 ml (8 fl oz) water
250 g (8 oz) wholemeal flour
25 g (1 oz) cocoa powder
½ **teaspoon grated nutmeg**
50 g (2 oz) ground almonds
1 teaspoon bicarbonate of soda
1 egg, beaten

Topping: (optional)
125 g (4 oz) skimmed milk soft
   cheese or curd cheese
125 g (4 oz) natural fromage frais
2 teaspoons clear honey
fine strands of orange rind

Grease and line a 20 cm (8 inch) cake tin. Place the sugar, margarine, carrots, raisins and water in a saucepan. Bring to the boil and boil for 5 minutes. Remove from the heat and allow to cool.

Mix the dry ingredients in a bowl, then make a well in the centre. Add the beaten egg and the contents of the saucepan, then beat well. Spoon the mixture into the prepared cake tin.

Bake the cake mixture in a preheated oven, 190°C (375°F), Gas Mark 5, for 40–50 minutes until firm and a skewer inserted in the centre comes out clean. Cool in the tin for 10 minutes, then invert the cake on to a wire rack to cool completely.

To make the topping, if using, beat the cheese until softened and add the fromage frais and honey. Mix well. Spread the topping over the cake and decorate with fine strands of orange rind.

Makes 12–15 slices

Granny's Iced Chocolate Sponge

175 g (6 oz) sunflower margarine
175 g (6 oz) caster sugar
2 eggs, beaten
200 g (7 oz) self-raising flour
25 g (1 oz) cocoa powder

left: chocolate, carrot and raisin cake, granny's iced chocolate sponge, walnut brownies

6 tablespoons milk
½ quantity Chocolate Buttercream Icing (see page 56)
walnut halves
chocolate buttons
glacé cherries, halved
Glacé Icing:
125 g (4 oz) icing sugar
1½ tablespoons boiling water

Grease and base-line 2 x 18 cm (7 inch) sandwich tins. Cream the margarine and sugar until pale and fluffy. Gradually beat in the eggs. Sift the flour and cocoa powder on to the mixture and fold in with the milk to form a soft dropping consistency.

Divide the mixture between the cake tins. Bake in a preheated oven, 180°C (350°F), Gas Mark 4, for 20–25 minutes until risen and firm. Invert on to a wire rack to cool.

Sandwich the cake layers together with the chocolate buttercream.

To make the glacé icing, sift the icing sugar into a bowl. Add the boiling water and mix well.

Spread the icing over the top of the sponge and decorate with walnut halves, chocolate buttons and glacé cherry halves.

Makes 10–12 slices

Walnut Brownies

125 g (4 oz) sunflower margarine
250 g (8 oz) muscovado sugar
2 eggs
1 teaspoon vanilla essence
50 g (2 oz) plain flour
25 g (1 oz) cocoa powder
½ teaspoon baking powder
50 g (2 oz) walnuts, chopped
1 tablespoon milk
½ quantity Chocolate Fudge Frosting (see page 34)
walnut pieces, to decorate

Grease and base-line an 18 cm (7 inch) square tin. In a bowl, cream the margarine and sugar together until they are pale and fluffy, then gradually beat in the eggs and vanilla essence.

Sift the flour, cocoa powder and baking powder together, then fold into the mixture with the walnuts and milk. Spoon into the cake tin and level the top.

Bake the brownie mixture in a preheated oven, 180°C (350°F), Gas Mark 4, for 30–35 minutes until firm to the touch. Leave in the tin for 5 minutes, then invert on to a wire rack to cool.

Spread the chocolate fudge frosting over the top of the brownie cake, swirling with a fork. Decorate with walnut pieces and cut the cake into bars to serve.

Makes 15 bars

Yogurt Chocolate Cake

150 ml (¼ pint) sunflower oil

125 g (4 oz) chocolate yogurt

5 tablespoons golden syrup

175 g (6 oz) caster sugar

3 eggs

250 g (8 oz) self-raising flour

25 g (1 oz) cocoa powder

½ teaspoon bicarbonate of soda

½ teaspoon salt

Topping:

125 g (4 oz) plain chocolate, broken
into pieces

25 g (1 oz) butter

2 teaspoons milk

white chocolate curls

Grease and base-line a 20 cm
(8 inch) cake tin. Place the oil,
yogurt, golden syrup, sugar and
eggs in a bowl and beat well. Sift
the flour, cocoa powder,
bicarbonate of soda and salt into
the bowl and mix thoroughly.

Pour into the cake tin and bake in
a preheated oven, 160°C (325°F),
Gas Mark 3, for 1½–1¾ hours until
a skewer inserted into the centre
comes out clean. Invert on to a wire
rack to cool.

Put the chocolate, butter and milk
in a heatproof bowl over a saucepan
of simmering water. Stir until the
chocolate has melted. Spread over
the cake and make patterns with a
fork. Decorate with chocolate curls.

Makes 8–10 slices

Banana Chocolate Slices

50 g (2 oz) sunflower margarine

50 g (2 oz) soft brown sugar

2 large ripe bananas, mashed

2 tablespoons cocoa powder

1 tablespoon drinking chocolate
powder

150 ml (¼ pint) natural yogurt

1 egg, beaten

175 g (6 oz) wholemeal flour

1½ teaspoons baking powder

½ teaspoon bicarbonate of soda

25 g (1 oz) crunchy oat cereal

1 tablespoon demerara sugar

Grease and base-line a 18 cm
(7 inch) square tin. In a bowl, cream
the margarine with the soft brown
sugar until pale and fluffy. Beat in
the bananas, cocoa powder,
drinking chocolate powder, yogurt
and egg, then stir in the flour,
baking powder and bicarbonate of
soda. Spoon the mixture into the
tin. Level the top and sprinkle with
the crunchy oat cereal and
demerara sugar.

Bake in a preheated oven, 180°C
(350°F), Gas Mark 4, for 40–45
minutes until just firm. Leave in the
tin for 5 minutes then invert on to a
wire rack to cool completely. Cut
into slices to serve.

Makes 18–20

No-cook Chocolate Cake

125 g (4 oz) butter

2 tablespoons golden syrup

1 tablespoon milk

125 g (4 oz) plain chocolate, broken
into pieces

250 g (8 oz) rustic biscuits, crushed

25 g (1 oz) sultanas

25 g (1 oz) raisins

50 g (2 oz) glacé cherries, chopped

40 g (1½ oz) unsalted peanuts,
chopped

½ quantity Chocolate Fudge Frosting
(see page 34)

Grease and base-line a 500 g (1 lb)
loaf tin. Put the butter, golden
syrup, milk and chocolate in a large
heatproof bowl over a saucepan of
gently simmering water. Stir until
the butter and chocolate have
melted. Remove from the heat, stir
in the biscuit crumbs and mix well.
Add the sultanas, raisins, glacé
cherries and peanuts. Mix again.

Spoon into the loaf tin, press
down well and chill for 1–2 hours.

Turn the cake on to a serving plate,
remove the lining paper, then spread
a thick layer of chocolate fudge
frosting over the top of the cake and
make swirls with a palette knife.

Makes 16 slices

*right: yogurt chocolate cake, banana
chocolate slices, no-cook chocolate
cake*

Biscuits and Festive Food

Coconut Chocolate Crispies

125 g (4 oz) milk chocolate, broken into pieces

2 tablespoons milk

2 tablespoons golden syrup

125 g (4 oz) rice pops

75 g (3 oz) desiccated coconut

Arrange 20 paper cake cases on a baking sheet.

Place the chocolate, milk and golden syrup in a bowl over a pan of simmering water. Stir until the chocolate has melted. Add the cereal and coconut and mix well.

Divide the mixture among the paper cake cases and leave to set.

Makes 20

Chocolate Chip Sesame Flapjacks

75 g (3 oz) sunflower margarine

3 tablespoons golden syrup

3 tablespoons plain chocolate drops

1 tablespoon sesame seeds

175 g (6 oz) porridge oats

Grease and base-line an 18 cm (7 inch) square cake tin. Place the margarine and syrup in a saucepan and heat gently until the margarine has melted. Remove from the heat and add the chocolate drops, sesame seeds and oats and mix well. Press into the cake tin.

Bake in a preheated oven, 160°C (325°F), Gas Mark 3, for 25 minutes. Leave in the tin for 10 minutes, then cut out 9–12 flapjacks and transfer to a wire rack to cool completely.

Makes 9–12

Chocolate Top Gingers

175 g (6 oz) wholemeal flour

50 g (2 oz) porridge oats

½ teaspoon bicarbonate of soda

1 teaspoon cream of tartar

2 teaspoons ground ginger

175 g (6 oz) margarine

175 g (6 oz) demerara sugar

200 g (7 oz) plain chocolate, melted

Grease a 28 x 18 cm (11 x 7 inch) Swiss roll tin. Put the flour, porridge oats, bicarbonate of soda, cream of tartar and ground ginger in a bowl. Rub in the margarine until the mixture resembles fine breadcrumbs. Stir in the sugar and press into the cake tin.

Bake in a preheated oven, 160°C (325°F), Gas Mark 3, for 30 minutes until lightly browned. Cool in the tin, then cover with the chocolate. When set, cut into fingers.

Makes 20

Right: coconut chocolate crispies, chocolate top gingers, chocolate chip sesame flapjacks

Chocolate Nut Cookies

250 g (8 oz) plain flour
1 teaspoon baking powder
125 g (4 oz) sunflower margarine
175 g (6 oz) caster sugar
50 g (2 oz) plain or milk chocolate drops
25 g (1 oz) chopped nuts
1 teaspoon vanilla essence
1 egg, beaten

Grease a baking sheet. Sift the flour and baking powder into a bowl. Rub in the margarine until the mixture resembles fine breadcrumbs. Stir in the sugar, chocolate drops and nuts. Add the vanilla essence and egg, then mix to a stiff dough.

Turn on to a floured surface and knead, then roll into a long sausage. Wrap in a sheet of foil, twisting the ends to seal. Roll the sausage backwards and forwards to form an even roll about 5 cm (2 inches) thick. Place in the refrigerator for several hours or overnight.

Cut the number of biscuits required and space out the baking sheet. Cook in a preheated oven, 190°C (375°F), Gas Mark 5, for 10–12 minutes. Leave on the baking sheet for 5 minutes, then transfer to a wire rack to cool completely. Store in an airtight container.

The roll of uncooked dough will keep in the refrigerator for 1 week.

Makes 50–60

Chocolate Date and Oat Fingers

175 g (6 oz) chopped dates
3 tablespoons water
50 g (2 oz) plain chocolate, melted
125 ml (4 fl oz) sunflower oil
1 tablespoon clear honey
25 g (1 oz) demerara sugar
125 g (4 oz) porridge oats
125 g (4 oz) wholemeal flour

Grease and line an 18 cm (7 inch) square cake tin. Simmer the dates and water in a pan for 5 minutes. Stir in the chocolate and set aside.

Mix the oil with the honey. Stir in the sugar, oats and flour. Place half of the mixture in the cake tin. Press down well, then cover with the date mixture. Top with the remaining oat mixture, pressing it down well.

Bake in a preheated oven, 190°C (375°F), Gas Mark 5, for 20–25 minutes. Cool in the tin for 5 minutes, cut into 12 fingers, then leave to cool completely in the tin.

Makes 12

Chocolate Crunch Wedges

75 g (3 oz) butter
2 tablespoons golden syrup
1 tablespoon soft brown sugar
1 tablespoon cocoa powder
250 g (8 oz) digestive biscuits, crushed
50 g (2 oz) raisins

Grease a 20 cm (8 inch) flan ring or loose-bottomed tin. Place the butter, golden syrup, sugar and cocoa powder in a saucepan and heat gently until the butter has melted.

Stir in the biscuit crumbs and raisins. Press the mixture into the ring or tin. Chill in the refrigerator until firm, then cut into wedges.

Makes 12–16

above: chocolate nut cookies, chocolate crunch wedges, chocolate date and oat fingers
right: florentines

Florentines

50 g (2 oz) butter

50 g (2 oz) caster sugar

25 g (1 oz) plain or wholemeal flour

40 g (1½ oz) glacé cherries, finely chopped

25 g (1 oz) stem ginger, finely chopped

25 g (1 oz) flaked almonds

25 g (1 oz) mixed peel, finely chopped

125 g (4 oz) plain chocolate, melted

Line a large baking sheet with 2 layers of nonstick baking paper. Place the butter and sugar in a heatproof bowl over a saucepan of gently simmering water. Stir until the butter has melted, then remove from the heat and add the flour. Mix until smooth, then stir in the glacé cherries, stem ginger, flaked almonds and mixed peel.

Place spoonfuls of the mixture well apart on the baking sheet. Bake in a preheated oven, 180°C (350°F), Gas Mark 4, for 8–10 minutes until golden. Leave to cool for 10 minutes, then, using a palette knife, carefully transfer the biscuits to a wire rack to cool completely.

Spread the melted chocolate over one side of each florentine and mark lines with a fork if wished. Leave to harden.

Makes 10–12

Chocolate Lemon Digestives

75 g (3 oz) wholemeal flour
pinch of salt
½ teaspoon baking powder
40 g (1½ oz) medium oatmeal
40 g (1½ oz) butter
25 g (1 oz) soft brown sugar
finely grated rind of ½ lemon
3 tablespoons milk
Topping:
1½ teaspoons lemon juice
50 g (2 oz) plain or milk chocolate,
   melted

Grease a baking sheet. Place the flour, salt, baking powder and oatmeal in a bowl. Rub in the butter until the mixture resembles fine breadcrumbs. Stir in the sugar and lemon rind. Add the milk and mix to a stiff biscuit dough. Turn on to a floured board and knead well. Roll out to a round just under 5 mm (¼ inch) thick.

Using a 7 cm (3 inch) plain cutter, cut out 12 biscuits, rolling the dough again as necessary. Place the biscuits on the baking sheet, allowing room for expansion.

Prick well and bake in a preheated oven, 190°C (375°F), Gas Mark 5, for 15–20 minutes until lightly browned. Transfer to a wire rack to cool.

Stir the lemon juice into the chocolate and spread over the biscuits. Mark lines over the chocolate before it sets.

Makes 12

Chocolate Shortbread

125 g (4 oz) butter, softened
50 g (2 oz) caster sugar
140 g (4½ oz) plain flour
20 g (¾ oz) cocoa powder
20 g (¾ oz) semolina
sifted icing sugar or 125 g (4 oz)
   white chocolate, melted, to
   decorate

Grease an 18 cm (7 inch) shortbread mould or sandwich tin. In a bowl, cream the butter with the sugar until pale and fluffy. Sift the flour and cocoa powder together and work into the butter mixture with the semolina. Press the mixture into the shortbread mould or sandwich tin and flatten the top. Use a fork to press down the edges.

Bake in a preheated oven, 160°C (325°F), Gas Mark 3, for 30–35 minutes. Mark into 8–10 pieces and leave to cool in the tin for 10 minutes, then transfer to a wire rack to cool completely.

Dust with icing sugar or spread with the melted white chocolate. Cut into wedges to serve.

Makes 8–10

left: chocolate lemon digestives, coconut caramel squares, chocolate shortbread
right: choc 'n' nut squares

Coconut Caramel Squares

75 g (3 oz) butter, melted

25 g (1 oz) drinking chocolate
  powder

125 g (4 oz) digestive biscuits,
  crushed

25 g (1 oz) desiccated coconut

Topping:

1 x 400 g (13 oz) can condensed milk

25 g (1 oz) butter

2 tablespoons golden syrup

1 tablespoon vanilla essence

50 g (2 oz) plain chocolate, broken
  into pieces

white chocolate curls, to decorate

Grease an 18 cm (7 inch) square
cake tin. In a bowl, mix the butter
with the drinking chocolate, biscuit
crumbs and coconut. Press into the
cake tin.

Place all the topping ingredients
in a saucepan and heat, stirring
until the chocolate and butter have
melted and the liquid begins to
boil. Boil for 4 minutes, stirring
vigorously, then pour over the
biscuit base and leave in a cool
place to set.

Cut into 16 squares and store in
an airtight container in the
refrigerator until required. To serve,
decorate with white chocolate curls.

Makes 16

Choc 'n' Nut Squares

175 g (6 oz) plain flour

2 tablespoons cocoa powder

75 g (3 oz) instant custard powder

175 g (6 oz) butter or block
  margarine

75 g (3 oz) caster sugar

Topping:

75 g (3 oz) butter

75 g (3 oz) dark brown sugar

1 tablespoon clear or set honey

125 g (4 oz) nuts, chopped and
  toasted

125 g (4 oz) plain or milk chocolate,
  melted (optional)

Grease and base-line an 18 cm
(7 inch) square cake tin with
greaseproof paper. Sift the flour and
cocoa into a large bowl. Add the
custard powder, then rub the butter
or margarine into the mixture until
it begins to become sticky.

Add the caster sugar and continue
rubbing until the mixture begins to
form a solid mass. Press into a ball
shape and knead lightly with a little
extra flour until smooth.

Press the dough into the base of
the cake tin to cover it, pushing
well into the corners. Prick the
surface with a fork.

Bake in a preheated oven,
150°C (300°F), Gas Mark 2, for
1¼–1½ hours until the mixture
begins to brown. Cool in the tin for
10 minutes, then carefully turn out.
Peel off the paper and cool on a
wire rack.

To make the topping, melt the
butter, sugar and honey in a small
heavy-based saucepan, over a low
heat, then boil for 3 minutes,
stirring constantly. Away from the
heat, stir in the nuts and spread the
mixture over the biscuit base. Leave
to set for about 15 minutes.

Cut the biscuit slab into about
20 equal squares and leave for about
30 minutes until firm.

Dip the top of each square
diagonally into the chocolate, if
using, and place on nonstick baking
paper to set.

Makes about 20

Chocolate Fudge

50 g (2 oz) butter

125 g (4 oz) plain chocolate, broken
   into pieces

5 tablespoons evaporated milk

1 teaspoon vanilla essence

500 g (1 lb) icing sugar, sifted

50 g (2 oz) chopped nuts, toasted
   (optional)

125 g (4 oz) plain chocolate, melted,
   to decorate

Butter an 18–20 cm (7–8 inch)
square tin.

   Place the butter, chocolate and
evaporated milk in a small
heatproof bowl set over a pan of hot
water. Stir vigorously until smooth.
Add the vanilla essence.

   Pour the chocolate mixture into
the icing sugar, and nuts, if using.
Beat until thoroughly blended.

   Press into the tin and leave in a
cool place to set.

   Spread the chocolate over the
fudge with a spatula. Roughen the
surface with a fork and leave until

set. Cut the fudge into squares.
Store in an airtight container for
3–4 days.

Makes 50–60

Variations:

Use milk or white chocolate for a milder
chocolate flavour, and replace the nuts
with an equal quantity of chopped
glacé cherries and chopped angelica.

*above: chocolate fudge, chocolate
stars, caramel crunch biscuits*

Chocolate Stars

125 g (4 oz) butter or margarine
200 g (7 oz) plain flour, sifted
25 g (1 oz) cornflour
75 g (3 oz) caster sugar
25 g (1 oz) drinking chocolate
  powder
grated rind of 1 orange
1 egg
Icing:
500 g (1 lb) icing sugar, sifted
4 tablespoons orange juice
few drops orange food colouring
2 tablespoons cocoa powder, sifted
2 tablespoons boiling water

Grease 2 baking sheets. Rub the butter or margarine into the flour and cornflour then add the sugar, drinking chocolate powder and orange rind. Stir well then add the egg. Mix to a smooth dough.

Lightly knead the dough and roll out on a floured work surface to about 5 mm (¼ inch) thick. Cut out star shapes using a cutter or cardboard template about 7 cm (3 inches) from point to point.

Bake in 2 batches on the baking sheets in a preheated oven, 180°C (350°F), Gas Mark 4, for about 15 minutes each batch until firm and golden. Cool on a wire rack.

To make the icing, blend the icing sugar with the orange juice. Spoon 3 tablespoons of the icing into a cup and mix with a little orange colouring, adding a little more icing sugar if necessary, to make a smooth piping consistency.

Spoon the orange icing into a small greaseproof paper icing bag and cut a very small hole to produce a fine line when piped.

Blend the cocoa with the boiling water, cool slightly, then mix with the remaining icing, adding a little more icing sugar, if necessary, to make a stiff coating consistency.

Coat the tops of 2–3 biscuits at a time with the chocolate icing and, while still wet, pipe about 4–5 circles of orange icing, starting in the centre. With a fine skewer, draw the orange icing from the centre outwards to each point, then draw inwards from the angle at the base of each point to the centre. Repeat until all the biscuits are coated. Leave to dry.

Makes about 24

Caramel Crunch Biscuits

125 g (4 oz) butter or margarine
25 g (1 oz) caster sugar
25 g (1 oz) drinking chocolate
  powder
1 teaspoon vanilla essence
175 g (6 oz) digestive biscuits,
  crushed
50 g (2 oz) chopped nuts (unsalted
  peanuts, hazelnuts, almonds,
  walnuts)
2nd layer:
1 x 400 g (13 oz) can condensed milk
25 g (1 oz) butter
3 tablespoons golden syrup
1 teaspoon vanilla essence
3rd layer:
125 g (4 oz) plain or milk chocolate,
  melted

Grease an 18 x 28 cm (7 x 11 inch) Swiss roll tin.

Melt the butter or margarine together with the sugar, drinking chocolate powder and vanilla essence in a saucepan over a low heat. Stir well.

Stir in the crushed digestive biscuits and chopped nuts until all the butter or margarine has been absorbed. Press the mixture into the bottom of the Swiss roll tin.

To make the second layer, put all the ingredients into a small heavy-based saucepan and heat gently until the mixture begins to bubble. Stir vigorously and continuously while the mixture boils gently for 3 minutes. A brown skin will form on the sides of the pan and this should be stirred in vigorously. Avoid allowing the mixture to burn.

Pour the caramel mixture over the biscuit base and spread evenly with a palette knife. To make the third layer, pour the chocolate over the caramel. Spread evenly and mark a pattern with the blunt side of a knife. Chill for about 2 hours until set. Mark the chocolate into 24 equal squares. Cut in the tin, using a sharp knife, and lift out each square with a palette knife.

Makes 24

Mushroom Cake

½ quantity Chocolate Victoria sponge
   mixture (see page 56)
1 quantity Chocolate Buttercream
   Icing (see page 56)
250 g (8 oz) marzipan
2 tablespoons seedless jam, warmed
icing sugar, for dusting

Grease a 20 cm (8 inch) square cake
tin. Spoon in the cake mixture and
bake in a preheated oven, 180°C
(350°F), Gas Mark 4, for 25–30
minutes. Turn out and cool on a
wire rack.

Using a piping bag fitted with a
large star nozzle, pipe lines of
buttercream from the edge of the
cake to the centre until the top is
covered.

Reserve 25 g (1 oz) of the
marzipan and roll the remainder
into a sausage about 60 cm
(24 inches) long, then roll a thin
strip that will cover and just stand
above the cake sides.

Brush the side of the cake with
the jam and press the strip on top.
Roll a clean, straight-sided jar
several times over the join to blend
it together. Push the marzipan that
is above the level of the side
inwards so that it curves slightly
over the piped ridges.

Shape the remaining marzipan
into a 'stalk' and place in the centre.
Dust the cake lightly with icing
sugar.

Serves 6

Variation:

Chocolate Butterflies
Divide the cake mixture between about
14–16 paper cases and bake in a
preheated oven, 190°C (375°F),
Gas Mark 5, for about 15–20 minutes
until well risen. When cold, cut a circle
from the top of each, using a sharp
knife. Cut each small circle in half.
Spoon or pipe a little buttercream into
the centre of each cake, using a star
nozzle, and press 2 semi-circular pieces
into it to look like butterfly wings. Dust
with icing sugar and top with halved
glacé cherries or nuts.

Tip: To measure the marzipan for the
cake exactly, cut 2 pieces of string,
1 x 5 mm (¼ inch) higher than the cake,
and the other the exact width around
the cake. Roll out the marzipan and trim
length and width to the size of the
string. Roll the marzipan into a coil and
place one end on the side of the cake.
Unroll carefully around the cake to
cover it evenly. Use a jam jar or small
palette knife to smooth the join.

Chocolate Finger Dips

200 g (7 oz) plain flour
25 g (1 oz) caster sugar
25 g (1 oz) fine semolina
25 g (1 oz) hazelnuts, finely ground
   (optional)
grated rind of 1 lemon
125 g (4 oz) butter or margarine
1 egg

Dip:

200 g (7 oz) milk chocolate, broken
   into pieces
25 g (1 oz) butter
125 ml (4 fl oz) milk, warmed
25 g (1 oz) hazelnuts, finely ground
   and toasted (optional)

Grease 2 baking sheets. Combine
the flour, sugar, semolina,
hazelnuts, if using, and lemon rind
in a bowl and rub in the fat until
the mixture resembles fine
breadcrumbs. Add the egg and mix
to a soft pliable dough. Knead
lightly on a floured work surface
until smooth.

Roll out the dough into a
rectangle 20 x 25 cm (8 x 10 inches)
and 5 mm (¼ inch) thick. Cut the
rectangle in half across its short
width, then cut each small rectangle
into sticks or fingers of dough about
1 cm (½ inch) wide.

Transfer to the baking sheets
and bake in a preheated oven,
180°C (350°F), Gas Mark 4, for
10–15 minutes until golden. Lift
on to a wire rack to cool.

To make the dip, melt the
chocolate and butter in a small
heatproof bowl over a saucepan of
hot water. Stir until thick and
smooth. Gradually add the milk,
beating well between each addition
until the dip is smooth and runny.
Stir in the nuts, if using.

Divide the dip between 6–8
individual, patterned waxed paper
cups, or pour into a small bowl, and
leave for about 1 hour until cold.
The dip will thicken on cooling.

Divide the biscuits into 6–8 equal bundles and wrap each with a napkin that matches the waxed paper cups, if using.

Serves 6–8

Surprise Cones

10 round ice cream cones
50 g (2 oz) unsalted mixed nuts, chopped and toasted
10 pink and white marshmallows
icing sugar, for tossing
4 tablespoons milk or evaporated milk, warmed
200 g (7 oz) milk chocolate, melted

25 g (1 oz) chocolate vermicelli or hundreds and thousands, to decorate

Prop up the ends of a wire rack so that the cones can sit upright, inserted into the tray.

Sprinkle a few chopped nuts into the bottom of each cone.

Snip the marshmallows into small pieces with scissors, toss in a little icing sugar to keep the pieces separate. Then stir in the remaining chopped nuts.

Gradually beat the warmed milk or evaporated milk into the chocolate until smooth. Set aside for about 30 minutes until cool but still soft.

Stir the marshmallow and nut mixture into the chocolate mixture and leave for about 1 hour until completely cold, but still sticky.

Just before serving, place 2 heaped teaspoons of the mixture in each cone and round the top.

Dip the top of each cone into the chocolate vermicelli or hundreds and thousands and serve immediately, before the cones start to soften.

Makes 10

above: mushroom cake, chocolate finger dips, surprise cones

71

Marble Ring Cake

175 g (6 oz) butter

175 g (6 oz) caster sugar

3 eggs

250 g (8 oz) self-raising flour

2 tablespoons cocoa powder

2 teaspoons instant coffee powder or granules

2 tablespoons hot water

½ teaspoon vanilla essence

½ teaspoon peppermint essence

a few drops green food colouring

icing sugar, for dusting

Grease a 1.5 litre (2½ pint) ring mould with butter.

Cream the butter and sugar until the mixture is very light and fluffy and has the appearance of whipped cream.

Beat in the eggs, 1 at a time; if the mixture looks as if it may curdle, beat in 1 tablespoon of the flour before the last egg. Sift the flour over the mixture and fold in lightly but thoroughly until evenly mixed.

Divide the mixture between 3 separate bowls. Blend the cocoa and coffee with the hot water. When cool, beat into one portion of mixture. Beat the vanilla essence into the second portion of mixture, and the peppermint essence and a few drops of green colouring into the remaining portion.

Spoon the mixtures alternately, 1 heaped tablespoon at a time, into the prepared ring mould. Draw a fine skewer through the mixture right around the ring mould twice, to blend the colours slightly.

Bake in a preheated oven, 180°C (350°F), Gas Mark 4, for 40–45 minutes until the cake is well risen and springs back when lightly pressed with the fingers. Turn out and cool on a wire rack.

When cold, dust lightly with icing sugar.

Serves 8–10

above: marble ring cake, chocolate fudge bars, peanut cookies
right: variety squares

Peanut Cookies

25 rectangular ice cream wafers

175 g (6 oz) plain chocolate, broken into pieces

40 g (1½ oz) butter

3 tablespoons golden syrup

1 x 400 g (13 oz) can condensed milk

4 tablespoons crunchy peanut butter

Line the base of a 28 x 18 cm (11 x 7 inch) Swiss roll tin with foil. Line the base of the tin with the ice cream wafers and trim where necessary to fit perfectly. Remove the wafers from the tin, then fit and trim the remaining wafers in the same way. Lift out and keep the 2 batches separate. Brush any crumbs from the tin.

Melt the chocolate and 15 g (½ oz) of the butter in a small heatproof bowl set over a saucepan of hot water. Stir vigorously until smooth. Spread half the chocolate mixture over the base of the foil-lined tin and cover with a layer of the wafers.

Melt the remaining butter, golden

syrup and condensed milk in a heavy-based saucepan. Heat gently until the mixture begins to bubble. Stir vigorously while the mixture boils for 3 minutes. Away from the heat, beat in the peanut butter. Continue beating until very thick, then spoon on to the wafer layer in the tin and smooth level.

Fit the remaining wafers over the fudge filling, pressing them down well, and spread the rest of the chocolate on top.

Chill for about 30 minutes until the chocolate has set. With a sharp knife, cut into 24 squares. Lift the cookies out of the tin and carefully peel off the foil.

Makes 24

Chocolate Fudge Bars

4 tablespoons golden syrup
125 g (4 oz) butter or block
    margarine
125 g (4 oz) plain chocolate, broken
    into pieces

250 g (8 oz) digestive biscuits or
    other plain, sweet biscuits, coarsely
    crushed
50 g (2 oz) shredded coconut or
    chopped nuts
50 g (2 oz) glacé cherries, quartered
50 g (2 oz) sultanas

Line the base of an 18 cm (7 inch) square cake tin with greased greaseproof paper. Spoon the syrup into a heavy-based saucepan and add the butter or margarine. Heat gently until both have melted, and stir well.

Away from the heat, add the chocolate and stir vigorously until well blended.

Stir the biscuit crumbs, coconut or nuts, cherries and sultanas into the chocolate mixture. Mix well.

Pour into the cake tin, spread evenly and press down firmly. Cool, then chill for about 3 hours until set.

Carefully turn out the fudge biscuit slab on to a chopping board and cut into approximately 15 bars. Keep chilled in warm weather.

Makes 15–20

Variety Squares

rice paper
250 g (8 oz) granulated sugar
250 g (8 oz) soft brown sugar
150 ml (¼ pint) water
2 egg whites
125 g (4 oz) desiccated coconut,
    toasted
125 g (4 oz) glacé cherries, quartered
25 g (1 oz) angelica, chopped
    (optional)
125 g (4 oz) plain chocolate, melted

Dampen the inside of a 20 cm (8 inch) square cake tin. Line the base with a sheet of rice paper.

In a heavy-based saucepan, heat the sugars and water very gently until dissolved, then boil to the soft crack stage on a sugar thermometer, 132°C–142°C (270°F–286°F).

Whisk the egg whites until stiff, then gradually beat in the syrup. When the mixture becomes very stiff, add the coconut, glacé cherries, and angelica, if using. Mix well, then pour into the tin. Cover with more rice paper and press down with a heavy weight.

Leave the nougat to stand or chill for at least 24 hours, then ease out of the tin and cut into squares.

Melt the chocolate in a small heatproof bowl set over a pan of hot water. Stir until smooth. Dip each piece of nougat halfway into the chocolate. Cool until set on nonstick baking paper.

Makes about 30

Chocolate Coconut Pyramids

2 large sheets rice paper or nonstick
  baking paper
1 x 385 g (12½ oz) can condensed
  milk
375 g (12 oz) unsweetened
  desiccated coconut
25 g (1 oz) drinking chocolate
  powder
50 g (2 oz) chocolate chips
To decorate (optional):
75 g (3 oz) plain or milk chocolate,
  melted
25 g (1 oz) desiccated or shredded
  coconut
about 7 glacé cherries, quartered

Line 2 large baking sheets with the
rice paper or nonstick baking paper.
Pour the condensed milk into a
bowl with the coconut, drinking
chocolate powder and chocolate
chips. Beat well until well mixed.

Spoon into 15 mounds each of
about 2 heaped teaspoons each,
on each baking sheet. Leave a gap
between each mound to allow
the mixture to spread a little
during cooking.

Bake in a preheated oven,
190°C (375°F), Gas Mark 5, for
about 15–20 minutes until evenly
tinged brown. The mixture will still
feel soft to press but will harden on
cooling.

Lift the pyramids on to a wire
rack to cool, roughly tearing the rice
paper between them. Tear the paper
away neatly when cold. If using
baking powder, lift the pyramids off
the paper on to a wire rack to cool.

To make the topping, if using,
swirl a little melted chocolate on
the top of each pyramid, sprinkle
over a little coconut and top with a
glacé cherry quarter. Leave for about
30 minutes to set.

Makes 30

Chocolate Treasure Cups

175–250g (6–8 oz) plain chocolate,
  melted
6 teaspoons strawberry or raspberry
  jam
3 trifle sponges, broken into small
  pieces
1 x 400 g (13 oz) can mandarin
  orange segments in natural juice,
  drained and juice reserved
2 teaspoons powdered gelatine
125 g (4 oz) red glacé cherries, or
  red, green and yellow mixed,
  chopped, washed and dried

Line a tray or baking sheet with
greaseproof paper. Using a
teaspoon, spread enough chocolate
into 6 individual aluminium foil
cases, 7 cm (3 inches) in diameter
and 5–6 cm (2–2½ inches) deep, to
coat the insides evenly. Invert each
case on to the greaseproof paper
and leave for about 20 minutes
until the chocolate is firm. Keep the
remaining chocolate liquid over hot
water.

When the chocolate-lined cases
are firm, repeat the coating layer
with the remaining chocolate and
invert on the greaseproof paper.
Leave for about 1 hour until
completely set.

Turn each case the right way up.
Place 1 teaspoon of jam in each
case.

Put the trifle sponge pieces in a
bowl.

Divide the mandarin segments into 2 portions and roughly chop them, cutting each segment into about 4 pieces. Combine 1 portion with the trifle sponge pieces.

Pour the juice into a small saucepan and sprinkle over the gelatine. Heat gently, without boiling, until dissolved. Pour over the sponge cake and stir well. Cool.

Spoon the sponge mixture into the chocolate cases. Smooth level, then chill about 1 hour until set. Release the filled chocolate cases from the foil containers by gently running a round-bladed knife between the chocolate and the case.

Spoon the reserved chopped mandarin segments over the cups and sprinkle with the chopped glacé cherries.

Serves 6

Chocolate Honey Toffee

250 g (8 oz) clear or set honey
50 g (2 oz) soft brown sugar
125 g (4 oz) butter
2 teaspoons ground cinnamon
75 g (3 oz) plain chocolate, melted

Grease an 18–20 cm (7–8 inch) square tin.

Place the honey and sugar in a heavy-based saucepan and heat gently, stirring constantly, until the sugar has dissolved.

Add the butter and stir until melted. Boil the mixture until the soft crack stage is reached on a sugar thermometer, 132°C–142°C (270°F–285°F). Alternatively, drop a little of the toffee into iced water. Remove from the water and gently stretch it between the fingers. It should form hard but elastic strands, and only feel slightly sticky.

Away from the heat, sprinkle in the cinnamon and beat thoroughly, then pour into the tin. Leave in a cool place until almost firm but still slightly soft. Mark into squares with a knife. When cold, break into squares.

Dip each piece of toffee into the chocolate. Leave the toffee on nonstick baking paper until set.

Makes about 36

*left: chocolate coconut pyramids, chocolate treasure cups, chocolate honey toffee; **above**: chocolate pond*

Chocolate Pond

1 x 150 g (5 oz) lime jelly
50 ml (2 fl oz) double cream, whipped
about 12 miniature chocolate eggs, unwrapped
coloured sugar flowers
50 g (2 oz) strip of angelica, cut into fine strips

Make up the jelly according to the instructions on the packet and set in a large, shallow dish.

Fit a piping bag with a fine writing nozzle and spoon in the cream. Pipe blobs for eyes and a mouth on 1 end of each egg. Stick on to the lime jelly with a large blob of cream.

Place coloured flowers in groups on the jelly.

Insert the angelica into the jelly to look like reeds. Chill before serving.

Serves 6–8

Chocolate Butterflies

125 g (4 oz) self-raising flour
pinch of salt
25 g (1 oz) drinking chocolate
  powder
1 teaspoon cocoa powder
50 g (2 oz) butter
50 g (2 oz) caster sugar
1 egg, beaten
3 tablespoons milk
3 drops vanilla essence
To decorate:
½ quantity Vanilla Buttercream Icing
  (see page 50)
chocolate triangles
grated chocolate

Put 12–14 paper cake cases on a baking sheet or grease 12–14 patty tins.Sift the flour, salt, drinking chocolate powder and cocoa powder into a bowl. Rub in the butter until the mixture resembles fine breadcrumbs. Stir in the sugar and make a well in the centre. Add the egg, milk and vanilla essence, then mix well.

Spoon into the paper cake cases or into the patty tins. Bake in a preheated oven, 190°C (375°F), Gas Mark 5, for 15–20 minutes. Cool the cakes on a wire rack. Pipe whirls of vanilla buttercream on top of the cakes. Arrange the chocolate triangles to resemble wings; sprinkle grated chocolate in between.

Makes 12–14

Marshmallow Nut Fudge

2 tablespoons milk
125 g (4 oz) marshmallows, chopped
50 g (2 oz) butter
50 g (2 oz) granulated or caster sugar
1 tablespoon drinking chocolate
  powder
125 g (4 oz) icing sugar, sifted
25 g (1 oz) chopped hazelnuts,
  toasted

Grease a 15 cm (6 inch) square tin. Put 1 tablespoon of the milk and the marshmallows in a saucepan. Heat gently until the marshmallows have melted. Spoon into a bowl and set aside.

Add the remaining milk to the saucepan with the butter, sugar and drinking chocolate powder. Heat gently, stirring, until the butter has melted and the sugar has dissolved. Boil for 5 minutes.

Remove from the heat and stir in the marshmallow mixture, icing sugar and hazelnuts. Transfer to the tin and spread evenly.

When hard, cut into squares.

Makes 25–30

Chocolate Hedgehogs

125 g (4 oz) butter, softened

125 g (4 oz) caster sugar

2 eggs, beaten

75 g (3 oz) self-raising flour

25 g (1 oz) cocoa powder

1 tablespoon milk

2 drops vanilla essence

1 quantity Chocolate Buttercream
   Icing (see page 56)

To decorate:

125 g (4 oz) chocolate-flavoured
   sugar strands

125 g (4 oz) chocolate mint sticks

36 silver balls

5 liquorice pieces from 1 packet of
   small liquorice allsorts

Grease 18 shallow patty tins. Make the sponge following the method for Chocolate Victoria Sponge (see page 56), but using the ingredients in quantities listed here. Spoon into the patty tins. Bake in a preheated oven, 180°C (350°F), Gas Mark 4 for 15–18 minutes until risen and firm. Leave in the tins for 5 minutes, then transfer the cakes to a wire rack to cool completely.

Slice off the top of each cake to make it flat, then place upside down on a board. Cover each cake with buttercream, shaping it to form a snout. Sprinkle with sugar strands. Cut the chocolate mint sticks into 1.5 cm (¾ inch) pieces and insert into the icing to make spikes. Place 2 silver balls above each snout for eyes. Cut each liquorice piece into 4, using each round as a nose. Place the hedgehogs on a serving plate.

Makes 18

*left: chocolate butterflies,
marshmallow nut fudge;
above: chocolate hedgehogs*

Chocolate Coconut Ice

300 ml (½ pint) milk
1 kg (2 lb) granulated sugar
250 g (8 oz) desiccated coconut
1 teaspoon cocoa powder

Grease a 20 cm (8 inch) square cake tin. Place the milk and sugar in a saucepan and heat gently, stirring, until the sugar dissolves. Bring to the boil, cover the pan and boil for 8–10 minutes, without stirring, until a sugar thermometer reads 115–116°C (238–240°F) or when a little of the mixture dropped into a cup of water forms a soft ball.

Remove from the heat. Add the coconut, beating well until thick and creamy. Pour half the mixture into the tin. Quickly beat the cocoa powder into the remaining mixture and spread over the white layer. When set, cut into squares or bars.

Makes about 60

Simple Chocolate Fudge

25 g (1 oz) butter
50 g (2 oz) plain chocolate, broken into pieces
2 tablespoons single cream
½ teaspoon vanilla essence
250 g (8 oz) icing sugar, sifted

Grease a small, shallow tray. Place the butter and chocolate in a heatproof bowl and set over a saucepan of hot water. Stir until the chocolate has melted.

Stir in the cream and vanilla essence. Gradually work in the icing sugar and mix well. Spoon into the tray and leave to set.

Cut into squares and store in an airtight container until required.

Makes 20

Chocolate Raisin Fudge

300 ml (½ pint) milk
125 g (4 oz) plain chocolate, broken into pieces
875 g (1¾ lb) golden granulated sugar
125 g (4 oz) butter
50 g (2 oz) raisins
2 teaspoons vanilla essence

Grease an 18 cm (7 inch) square tin. Place the milk and chocolate in a saucepan and heat gently until the chocolate has melted. Add the sugar and butter and continue to heat, stirring, until the sugar has dissolved.

Bring to the boil, cover and boil for 2 minutes. Remove the lid and boil without stirring for 10–15 minutes until a sugar thermometer reads 115–116°C (238–240°F) or when a little of the mixture dropped into a cup of cold water forms a soft ball.

Remove from the heat and stir in the raisins and vanilla essence. Cool for 5–10 minutes. Beat the fudge until it loses its gloss, then spoon into the tin. When set, cut into neat squares.

Makes about 50

left: chocolate coconut ice, simple chocolate fudge
above: *chocolate raisin fudge*

Chocolate Peppermint Creams

25 g (1 oz) butter
1 tablespoon single cream
250 g (8 oz) icing sugar
2 teaspoons cocoa powder
½ teaspoon peppermint essence
sifted icing sugar, for dusting

Place the butter and cream in a heatproof bowl and set over a saucepan of gently simmering water. Stir until the butter has melted.

Sift the icing sugar and cocoa powder together, then work into the butter and cream with the peppermint essence. When cool enough to handle, knead until smooth, then turn on to a surface that is lightly dusted with icing sugar.

Divide the mixture in half and roll each piece to a cylinder about 15 cm (6 inches) long. Cut each into 15 slices and arrange in individual sweet cases or a lined box. Store the peppermints in a airtight container until required.

Makes about 30

above: chocolate peppermint creams
right: wicked coconut mallows, truffles

Wicked Coconut Mallows

desiccated coconut, for sprinkling
40 g (1½ oz) butter
2 tablespoons milk
250 g (8 oz) Devon toffees
75 g (3 oz) plain chocolate, broken into pieces
125 g (4 oz) icing sugar, sifted
125 g (4 oz) marshmallows, chopped
50 g (2 oz) unsalted peanuts

Sprinkle 2 sheets of greaseproof paper generously with desiccated coconut. Mix the butter, milk, toffees and chocolate in a heatproof bowl, then place over a saucepan of gently simmering water. Stir until melted, then remove from the heat and stir in the icing sugar, marshmallows and peanuts.

Tip half the mixture on to each sheet of greaseproof paper so that each forms a rough rectangle. Using the paper, roll each into a sausage shape about 3.5 cm (1½ inches) in diameter. Wrap in foil. Refrigerate for 2 hours, then cut into slices. Cover and refrigerate until required.

Makes 50–60

Truffles

50 g (2 oz) trifle sponges
175 g (6 oz) plain chocolate, melted
50 g (2 oz) butter, melted
1 tablespoon brandy or rum
2 egg yolks, beaten
50 g (2 oz) icing sugar, sifted
chocolate-flavoured sugar strands or sifted cocoa powder, for coating

Make the trifle sponges into fine crumbs by placing them in a blender or food processor, or by rubbing between the fingertips. Set aside.

In a bowl, mix together the chocolate, butter, brandy or rum, and the egg yolks. Stir in the reserved crumbs with the icing sugar, then mix well. Place the mixture in the refrigerator for about 30 minutes until it is firm enough to handle.

Roll teaspoonfuls of the mixture into balls in the palm of the hand. Toss each truffle in chocolate-flavoured sugar strands or cocoa powder and store in a covered container until required.

Makes 35–40

Party Cakes

Castle Cake

Make the flags for this cake by folding self-adhesive labels over cocktail sticks. Draw with a felt tip pen or stick coloured paper on the flags to make designs.

1 x 23 cm (9 inch) square cake (see page 50)
3 quantities Chocolate Fudge Frosting (see page 34)
4 mini milk chocolate Swiss rolls
about 60 milk chocolate finger biscuits
2 after dinner mints
4 flags, toy soldiers and birthday candles, to decorate

Slice the cake in half horizontally and spread with a thin layer of chocolate fudge frosting. Replace the top half and cover the cake with the remaining frosting. Mark lines across the top with a fork, first in one direction, then at right angles.

Place the cake on a square cake board. Place the mini chocolate Swiss rolls on end at each corner to make the turrets. Press chocolate fingers up the sides of the cake (trimming them to size, if necessary). Leave a space for the door on one side.

Make the door from an after dinner mint and 2 entire chocolate fingers, placed so that they are in line with the other biscuits. Place the other after dinner mint flat on the board in front of the door to make a drawbridge.

Decorate with flags, soldiers and birthday candles.

Makes 18–20 pieces

Keyboard Cake

250 g (8 oz) butter
250 g (8 oz) caster sugar
4 eggs, beaten
190 g (6½ oz) self-raising flour
3 tablespoons cocoa powder
1½ tablespoons milk
4 drops vanilla essence
To decorate and finish:
2 quantities Chocolate Buttercream Icing (see page 56)
8 sponge fingers
liquorice strips
small liquorice allsorts
birthday candles, as required

Grease and base-line a 30 x 23 cm (12 x 9 inch) roasting tin. Make the sponge cake following the instructions for Chocolate Victoria Sponge (see page 56), but using the ingredients in quantities listed here. Spoon the mixture into the tin. Level the top and make a slight hollow in the centre. Bake in a preheated oven, 190°C (375°F), Gas Mark 5, for 30–40 minutes until risen and a skewer inserted in the centre comes out clean. Invert on to a wire rack to cool.

Place the cake on a board and trim the edges. Cut a strip 6 cm (2½ inches) wide from the long side of the cake. Cut the larger piece of

cake in half horizontally and sandwich the 2 halves together with a thin layer of buttercream. Turn the strip on end and attach with buttercream to the back of the cake. Cover the whole cake with the remaining buttercream.

Place the sponge fingers on the cake to make the white keys. Cut the liquorice strips and position between the sponge fingers for the black keys. Cut sections from small liquorice allsorts and position to the side and behind the keys for buttons and controls.

Position birthday candles along the back section. Serve the cake on a foil-lined tray or rectangular cake board.

Makes 24–28 pieces

Chocolate Rabbit

175 g (6 oz) plain flour
25 g (1 oz) cocoa powder
1 teaspoon baking powder
1 teaspoon bicarbonate of soda
pinch of salt
125 g (4 oz) caster sugar
75 g (3 oz) sunflower margarine
150 ml (¼ pint) milk
2 eggs
1 tablespoon black treacle
To decorate and finish:
2 quantities Chocolate Buttercream
   Icing (see page 56)
125 g (4 oz) white marzipan

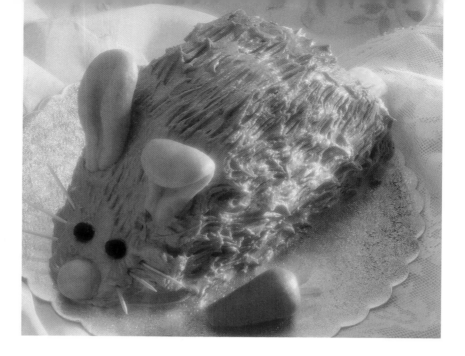

pink food colouring
orange food colouring
angelica
1 liquorice sweet, halved
cocktail sticks, halved

Grease and base-line a 20 cm (8 inch) round cake tin. Sift the first 5 ingredients into a bowl, stir well, then add the sugar, margarine, milk, eggs and treacle. Beat well for 2–3 minutes. Spoon into the tin. Bake in a preheated oven, 160°C (325°F), Gas Mark 3, for 30–40 minutes until firm and a skewer inserted into the centre comes out clean. Invert on to a wire rack to cool.

Cut the cake in half vertically to form 2 semi-circles. Sandwich together with one-quarter of the buttercream, then stand the cake on end, with the rounded side uppermost. Trim one end to form a snout. Cover the cake with the rest of the buttercream, using it to shape the snout – smooth this area with a palette knife. Roughen the buttercream elsewhere on the rabbit. Place on a cake board.

Roll one-third of the marzipan into a ball for the tail. Mark with a fork to give a fluffy appearance, then attach to the back of the rabbit. Add a few drops of pink and orange food colouring to the remaining marzipan and knead until evenly coloured. Roll a small piece into a ball to form the nose. Place this at the end of the snout and flatten slightly. Shape 2 equal-sized pieces of marzipan into rabbit ears about 5 cm (2 inches) long. Press into position on the head.

Add a few more drops of orange colouring to the marzipan. Knead well and shape like a carrot. Stick thin strips of angelica into the wider end to form the greenery. Place the carrot beside the rabbit.

Use the liquorice to make eyes. Place the cocktail sticks in position for whiskers.

Makes 15–20 pieces

left: castle cake, keyboard cake
above: chocolate rabbit

Ozzy Owl

If brown food colouring is not available, mix a little red and green colouring to make brown. It is important to use a true scarlet red and not cochineal.

1 quantity Chocolate Buttercream
   Icing (see page 56)
1 round ice cream cone
150 g (5 oz) yellow marzipan
brown food colouring
25 g (1 oz) white chocolate
250 g (8 oz) dark chocolate buttons
Quick Chocolate Cake:
200 g (7 oz) self-raising flour
25 g (1 oz) cocoa powder
250 g (8 oz) soft margarine
250 g (8 oz) caster sugar
4 eggs

Grease an ovenproof 600 ml (1 pint) pudding basin and an ovenproof 900 ml (1½ pint) pudding basin and cut 2 discs of greaseproof paper to line the base of each. Sift the flour and cocoa powder into a bowl and add the margarine, sugar and eggs. Beat thoroughly with a wooden spoon until the mixture is smooth and blended. Two-thirds fill each basin and level the surfaces. Bake the small cake in a preheated oven 160°C (325°F), Gas Mark 3, for about 45 minutes, and the larger cake for 1¼ hours, until they are well risen and spring back when pressed. Turn out, remove the paper and cool on a wire rack.

Slice both cakes in half horizontally and sandwich back together with a little of the buttercream.

Place the large cake, flat side down, on a cake board and sandwich the small cake, flat side down, on top with buttercream.

Transfer the cakes to a round serving dish or cakeboard. Reserve about 3 tablespoons of the buttercream and use the rest to cover the cakes completely. Stand on a round cake board or plate.

Cut the ice cream cone about 5 cm (2 inches) from the top and discard the tip end. Cut the remainder of the cone in half along its length. Using a sharp knife, trim each thin end of the cone to a point to make ears. Cover with some of the buttercream and stick on top of the cakes.

Divide the marzipan into 75 g (3 oz) and 50 g (2 oz) pieces. Colour the small piece brown and use about one-quarter to shape into a small hooked beak. Make 2 claws with 3 toes on each with the remainder.

Halve the yellow marzipan, knead until smooth, then shape into 2 thick ovals to form wings. Press these on to either side of the lower body and curve them away from the body at the top so there is a small hollow space between the wing and the body. Cover with the remaining buttercream.

Draw 2 oval shapes on greaseproof paper about the size of a large egg. Spread the white chocolate in the ovals and place a chocolate button in each to make eyes. Make sure the buttons are in the same position so that the eyes look in the same direction. Cool until set.

Place a row of chocolate buttons around the base of the owl, then place another row above so the buttons just overlap. Continue to layer the rows of buttons until the whole owl is covered, just leaving the face free.

Carefully lift the eyes off the paper and press into place. Position the beak and claws.

Makes 8–10 slices

Thomas Toad

1 quantity Quick Chocolate Cake
   (see left)
1 quantity Chocolate Buttercream
   Icing (see page 56)
50 g (2 oz) chocolate vermicelli
2 chocolate dome-shaped
   marshmallow cakes
25 g (1 oz) desiccated coconut
blue food colouring
125 g (4 oz) yellow marzipan
green food colouring
red food colouring
a little icing sugar

Make and bake the cake as for Ozzy Owl, on this page, and cut and sandwich them together with buttercream as instructed.

Reserve 1 tablespoon of buttercream and, using a palette knife, coat the cakes with the rest.

Cover with chocolate vermicelli.

Use the reserved buttercream to stick the marshmallow cakes on top at a slight angle to make eyes.

Using a sharp knife, make a slit about halfway down the side of the top cake, underneath the eyes, to make a mouth. Make the cut deep, slanting down to the bottom of the cake, so that the mouth will open gently. Secure the open mouth with a cocktail stick.

Mix the desiccated coconut with a little blue food colouring and spread over the cake board around the toad. This is the pond.

Divide the marzipan into two-thirds and one-third. Colour the large portion green. Halve the small portion, and colour one piece red.

Mould the red piece to rest in the base of the mouth. Shape 9 discs with the green marzipan and place in groups of 3 around the toad to represent leaves.

Shape 3 small thick discs with the yellow marzipan and using scissors snip small triangles out of the edge of the discs to look like water lilies. Close up slightly and position on the leaves.

Make up a little thick white icing with some icing sugar and water. Dab a little on both eyes and in the centre of each water lily.

Makes 8–10 slices

right: ozzy owl, thomas toad

Around the World

Danish Chocolate Pudding

3 dessert apples, peeled, cored and
   sliced
2 large ripe pears, peeled, cored and
   sliced
1 tablespoon water
25 g (1 oz) granulated sugar
   (optional)
50 g (2 oz) butter
150 g (5 oz) fresh wholemeal
   breadcrumbs
25 g (1 oz) brown sugar
25 g (1 oz) drinking chocolate
   powder
1 large chocolate flake bar, crumbled,
   to decorate

Place the apples, pears and water in
a saucepan. Stir in the sugar, if
using, and heat gently for
10 minutes until the fruit is soft.

Melt the butter in a saucepan over
a gentle heat. Stir in the
breadcrumbs, brown sugar and
drinking chocolate powder. Stir over
a moderate heat for 10–15 minutes
until the mixture becomes toasted
and has a crisp texture.

Layer the fruit and crumbs in a
600 ml (1 pint) dish, finishing with
a layer of crumbs. Sprinkle the
chocolate flake bar over the top.
Serve cold with Chocolate Sauce
(see page 19), natural yogurt or
single cream.

Serves 4

Chocolate Pavlova

The Pavlova is a dish of Australian
origin, created in honour of the famous
ballerina. The centre is lightly hollowed
out and built up at the sides to suggest
the dancer's tu-tu. Here it is adapted to
make the best of English summer fruit.

3 egg whites
250 g (8 oz) caster sugar
25 g (1 oz) cornflour
25 g (1 oz) cocoa powder
1 teaspoon lemon juice or vinegar
300 ml (½ pint) double or whipping
   cream, whipped
50 g (2 oz) plain chocolate, grated
few drops vanilla essence
250 g (8 oz) fresh strawberries,
   raspberries or loganberries
icing sugar, for sprinkling

Draw a 20 cm (8 inch) circle on
nonstick baking paper and place on
a baking sheet.

Whisk the egg whites until
standing in stiff peaks. Add 125 g
(4 oz) of the caster sugar and whisk
again until the mixture looks glossy
and stands in stiff peaks.

Sift the cornflour and cocoa
powder on to the meringue and fold
in lightly but thoroughly, together
with the remaining caster sugar, and
the lemon juice or vinegar.

Spoon the meringue into the circle on the baking paper. Spread the meringue evenly, then slightly scoop out the centre and build up the meringue towards the edge of the circle.

Bake in a preheated oven, 110°C (225°F), Gas Mark ¼, for 2½–3 hours until the meringue is crisp on the outside. Carefully lift off the paper and cool on a wire rack.

Fold the cream, grated chocolate and vanilla essence together and spoon into the centre of the meringue. Spread almost to the edge and top with the fruit. Sprinkle with icing sugar just before serving. Once filled, the meringue is best eaten on the same day.

Serves 4–6

Viennese Chocolate Whirls

250 g (8 oz) butter or block
  margarine, softened
50 g (2 oz) icing sugar
½ teaspoon vanilla essence
250 g (8 oz) plain flour
25 g (1 oz) drinking chocolate
  powder
50 g (2 oz) cornflour
To decorate:
125 g (4 oz) plain chocolate,
  melted
icing sugar, to dust

Grease 2 baking sheets. Cream the butter and icing sugar together until light and fluffy. Add the vanilla essence and beat well.

Sift the flour, drinking chocolate power and cornflour over the mixture and whisk until smooth.

Fill a large piping bag fitted with a 1.5 cm (¾ inch) star nozzle and pipe 'S' shapes on to the baking sheets.

Bake in a preheated oven, 180°C (350°F), Gas Mark 4, for about 25 minutes until golden. Leave for 2–3 minutes, then lift on to a wire rack to cool.

Leave the bowl of melted chocolate over the saucepan of hot water. Dip each biscuit halfway into the chocolate and leave on nonstick baking paper or greaseproof paper until set.

Line up the biscuits with the chocolate ends in one direction. Cover the chocolate loosely with a sheet of greaseproof paper and dust the uncovered ends with icing sugar. Store in an airtight container for 2–3 days.

Makes about 20

Left: danish chocolate pudding;
Above: chocolate pavlova, viennese chocolate whirls

Creole Cake

50 g (2 oz) dried apricots, finely
  chopped
4 tablespoons dark rum
50 g (2 oz) unsweetened desiccated
  coconut
1 tablespoon warm water
1 quantity Chocolate Victoria Sponge
  mixture (see page 56)

Fillings:
125 g (4 oz) plain chocolate, broken
  into pieces
15 g (½ oz) butter
25 g (1 oz) unsweetened desiccated
  coconut
1 tablespoon instant coffee powder
  or granules
1 tablespoon soft brown sugar
4 tablespoons boiling water
4 tablespoons apricot jam

300 ml (½ pint) double or whipping
  cream, whipped
chocolate caraque, to decorate

Soak the apricots in the rum for at
least 4 hours.

Grease 2 x 18 cm (7 inch) square
sandwich tins. Stir the coconut and
water into the sponge mixture and
divide between the tins. Bake in a
preheated oven, 190°C (375°F), Gas
Mark 5, for 25 minutes. Turn out on
to a wire rack to cool.

Cut 1 cake in half horizontally.

Put the chocolate and butter in a
small heatproof bowl and set over a
pan of hot water until melted. Stir
in the coconut.

In a second bowl, blend the
coffee, sugar and water.

Crumble the uncut cake into fine
crumbs, into a bowl. Spoon one-

third into the rum and apricots,
one-third into the chocolate and
the remainder into the coffee syrup.

Put 1 cut layer of cake on a
serving plate, cut-side up, and
spread 2 tablespoons of the jam
over the top. Spread the rum and
apricot mixture evenly over the
jam, then add the chocolate
mixture and lastly the coffee
mixture. Spread the remaining jam
over the remaining cake layer and
press, jam-side down, on to the
layers of filling. Spread the cream
evenly over the cake. Decorate with
chocolate caraque.

Serves 8

above: creole cake, danish spice cake,
English posset

Danish Spice Cake

250 g (8 oz) butter or block
  margarine
250 g (8 oz) caster sugar
300 g (10 oz) plain flour, sifted
25 g (1 oz) cocoa powder
2 teaspoons ground allspice
50 g (2 oz) plain chocolate
125 g (4 oz) chopped nuts (almonds,
  hazelnuts or walnuts), toasted
300 ml (½ pint) double or whipping
  cream

Cream the butter or margarine and sugar until light and fluffy. Beat in the flour, cocoa powder and allspice until a smooth dough is formed. Divide into 6 equal pieces.

Place each piece between 2 sheets of greaseproof or nonstick baking paper and roll out to a 20 cm (8 inch) round, using a template or sandwich tin as a guide. Remove the top layer of paper and transfer each round to a baking sheet. Prick all over with a fork. Bake in 3 batches of 2 baking sheets in a preheated oven, 220°C (425°F), Gas Mark 7, for about 6 minutes until browned. Remove from the baking sheets but leave on the paper. Trim while still warm, then cool on a wire rack.

Melt the chocolate in a small heatproof bowl set over a pan of hot water. Stir until smooth, then spread the chocolate over the surface of one round and scatter over a quarter of the nuts.

Just before serving, whip the cream and combine the remaining nuts with the cream. Carefully peel the paper off the pastry rounds and sandwich the layers together with the cream, ending with the coated round, chocolate uppermost.

Serves 8–10

English Posset

300 ml (½ pint) double cream, chilled
3 tablespoons drinking chocolate
  powder
1 tablespoon caster sugar
½ teaspoon ground cinnamon
2–3 tablespoons gin
50 g (2 oz) plain chocolate curls

Pour the cream into a chilled bowl and whip until it just holds it shape on the whisk. Add the drinking chocolate powder, sugar and cinnamon and whisk in gently.

Whisk in the gin to taste, 1 tablespoon at a time, taking care not to overwhip the cream. If necessary, fold in the last tablespoon with a metal spoon. Spoon into tall glasses and top with the chocolate curls. Chill overnight.

Serves 4–6

Finnish Gâteau

1 quantity Ganache Torte cake
  mixture (see page 44)
2 tablespoons instant custard powder
2 tablespoons caster sugar
300 ml (½ pint) milk
250 ml (8 fl oz) apple purée
175 g (6 oz) sugar
2 tablespoons cocoa powder
300 ml (½ pint) single cream
1½ tablespoons golden syrup
75 g (3 oz) butter, softened
25 g (1 oz) chopped almonds, toasted

Prepare and bake the cake as on page 44, to the end of step 3.

Blend the custard powder and sugar with a little of the cold milk and bring the remainder to the boil. Pour over the custard, stir well and return to the rinsed pan. Bring to the boil and cook for 2–3 minutes. Cover and cool. Beat the custard well. On a serving dish, sandwich the cake layers together with custard and apple purée.

Combine the sugar, cocoa, cream and syrup in a heavy-based saucepan and stir over a low heat until the sugar has dissolved. Bring to the boil, then boil gently until the mixture reaches 113–118°C (234–245°F) on a sugar thermometer. Cool until soft and very thick. Beat the butter gradually into the icing mixture. Spread the icing over the gâteau and coat the sides with chopped almonds.

Serves 8–10

Chocolate Bakewell Tart

175 g (6 oz) plain flour
pinch of salt
40 g (1½ oz) butter or margarine,
  chopped

40 g (1½ oz) lard or white fat
1½ tablespoons water
Filling:
2–3 tablespoons raspberry jam
50 g (2 oz) butter or margarine
50 g (2 oz) caster sugar
1 egg
50 g (2 oz) ground almonds
50 g (2 oz) cake crumbs

2 tablespoons cocoa powder, sifted
few drops almond essence
25 g (1 oz) flaked almonds (optional)

Grease an 18 x 28 cm (7 x 11 inch)
Swiss roll tin. Sift the flour and salt
into a bowl, then rub in the butter
or margarine until the mixture
resembles breadcrumbs.

Add the cold water and mix with a round-bladed knife, then combine with the fingers to bind the dough into a ball. Knead the pastry lightly on a floured surface. Roll out the pastry and use to line the Swiss roll tin. Prick the pastry with a fork. Spread the jam over the pastry.

Cream the butter or margarine and sugar until light and fluffy. Beat in the egg. Fold in the ground almonds, cake crumbs, cocoa and almond essence to taste. Spread the mixture over the jam and sprinkle with the flaked almonds, if using.

Bake in a preheated oven, 180°C (350°F), Gas Mark 4, for about 25 minutes. Cool on a wire rack then cut into rectangular pieces.

The tart will keep for up to 5 days in an airtight container.

Makes 12 slices

Rum Truffles

1 teaspoon instant coffee granules
1 tablespoon hot water
250 g (8 oz) plain chocolate, chopped
75 g (3 oz) butter, cut into pieces
1 tablespoon cream
2 tablespoons rum
1½ quantities crushed Praline (see right)
75–125 g (3–4 oz) chocolate vermicelli

left: rum truffles, chocolate bakewell tart

Dissolve the coffee granules in the hot water. Place the coffee and chocolate in a small heatproof bowl set over a pan of hot water. Stir until the mixture becomes smooth and thick.

Gradually add the butter, beating well between each addition, then stir in the cream, rum and praline. Cool in the bowl for 5–6 hours until firm.

Divide the mixture into 20 equal pieces and roll them between your hands to form neat shapes.

Pour the vermicelli into a wide shallow dish or plate and roll each truffle in them until well coated. Serve in paper cases. Keep cool.

Makes about 20

Praline

butter, for greasing
125 g (4 oz) caster sugar
125 g (4 oz) unskinned almonds

Grease a heatproof plate, tin or marble slab with butter.

Heat the sugar in a heavy-based pan over a low heat until it caramelizes. Try to avoid stirring the sugar at this stage, though this may become necessary if the sugar becomes over-heated.

Add the nuts and stir until they are toasted on both sides, then pour on to the heatproof plate. When the praline is completely cold, break it into pieces.

Devil's Food Cake

1 quantity Chocolate Victoria Sponge mixture (see page 56)
icing sugar, for dusting
Syrup:
250 ml (8 fl oz) water
125 g (4 oz) brown sugar
2 tablespoons cocoa powder
4 tablespoons rum
Filling:
125 g (4 oz) plain chocolate, melted
2 tablespoons cream
few drops vanilla essence
1 egg, beaten

Prepare and bake the sponge mixture in two greased and lined 20 cm (8 inch) tins in a preheated oven, 190°C (375°F), Gas Mark 5, for 20 minutes. Turn out and cool on a wire rack.

To make the syrup, combine the water, sugar, cocoa powder and rum in a small pan and heat gently until dissolved. Replace the cakes in the tins. Make a few holes in the cakes with a skewer and pour over the syrup. Soak for 2–3 hours.

To make the filling, stir the chocolate with the cream, vanilla and egg until smooth. Leave to cool until firm enough to spread, then use to sandwich the cakes together. Dust the top with icing sugar.

Makes 8–10 slices

Bûche de Noël

1 x 450 g (14½ oz) can sweetened
  chestnut purée
125 g (4 oz) unsalted butter, softened
250 g (8 oz) plain chocolate, broken
  into pieces
50 ml (2 fl oz) brandy or water
75 g (3 oz) caster sugar
1 teaspoon vanilla essence
To decorate:
2 glacé cherries
angelica
icing sugar

Line a 2 lb (1 kg) loaf tin with a
large sheet of buttered greaseproof
paper or foil, allowing plenty of
overhang. Mash the purée in a bowl
until smooth, then beat in the
butter.

Melt the chocolate with the
brandy or water in a small
heatproof bowl set over a saucepan
of hot water. Stir vigorously until
smooth, then gradually beat into
the chestnut mixture.

Add the sugar and vanilla essence
to the mixture and mix until
thoroughly blended.

Spoon the mixture into the loaf
tin and chill in the refrigerator until
it begins to harden. Lift the paper or
foil with the mixture out of the tin.
Roll the paper or foil over the
mixture and work into a long round
length to represent a log. Chill for
at least 6 hours.

To serve, unwrap the log and
place on a suitable serving dish.
Draw a fork over the surface to
roughen it and decorate with
halved glacé cherries and strips of
angelica. Keep chilled. Dust lightly
with icing sugar just before serving.

Serves 4–6

Colettes

To keep the cases rigid, use a double
layer of petit-four paper cases or a single
foil petit-four case.

125 g (4 oz) plain chocolate, melted
Filling:
1 teaspoon instant coffee powder or
  granules
1 tablespoon hot water
150 g (5 oz) plain chocolate, melted
2 tablespoons single or double cream
50 g (2 oz) butter, cut into small
  pieces
2 egg yolks
1–2 tablespoons rum
crystallized violets, chopped, to
  decorate

Leave the chocolate in the bowl
over the saucepan of hot water.
Spoon a little chocolate into each of
about 15 petit-four cases. With a
teaspoon, line the cases with half
the chocolate. When set, use the
remaining melted chocolate to coat
the chocolate cases again. Cool
until firm.

To make the filling, dissolve the
coffee in the hot water, then mix
with the chocolate and cream. Stir
until smooth and thick.

Away from the heat, gradually
add the butter, beating well after
each addition. When melted, beat
in the egg yolks and rum. Leave the
filling for about 3–4 hours until
cool and thick.

Carefully peel the paper or foil
cases away from the chocolate and
spoon or pipe in the filling using a
large star nozzle. Decorate each
colette with crystallized violet.

Makes about 15

Pacific Gold

1 small-medium pineapple
1 quantity Edwardian Rum Ice Cream
  (see page 30)
2 egg whites
125 g (4 oz) caster sugar
½ teaspoon vanilla essence

Carefully remove the top and
bottom of the pineapple. Reserve
the top and cut away any skin from
around the leaves. Peel the
pineapple and remove the eyes.

Cut the pineapple into about
4–6 slices and remove the core.

Beat the ice cream thoroughly,
then sandwich 2 slices of pineapple
together with the ice cream and fill
the centre with more ice cream.
Continue sandwiching the slices of
pineapple to make a whole fruit.

Whisk the egg whites until very
stiff, then add half the caster sugar.
Continue whisking until the
meringue is stiff and glossy, then

fold in the remaining sugar and the vanilla essence. Spoon into a large piping bag fitted with a 1.5 cm (¾ inch) star nozzle and cover the pineapple with stars.

Bake in a preheated oven, 240°C (475°F), Gas Mark 9, for about 3 minutes until the meringue points are tinged with brown all over.

Remove from the oven and push the reserved leaves into position on top of the meringue pineapple. Serve immediately or within 30 minutes.

Serves 4

above: bûche de noël, colettes, pacific gold

Russian Cake

6 tablespoons sherry

few drops red food colouring

5 tablespoons strawberry jam

375 g (12 oz) Madeira cake, cut into
fingers

icing sugar, for sprinkling

175 g (6 oz) marzipan

125 g (4 oz) plain chocolate, broken
into pieces

15 g (½ oz) butter

icing sugar for dusting (optional)

Grease a 500 g (1 lb) loaf tin.
Combine the sherry with a few
drops of red food colouring.

Using 4 tablespoons of the jam,
coat one side of each cake strip
thinly, then layer in the loaf tin
until half filled. Sprinkle with half
the sherry mixture.

Continue layering until the cake
has been used. Sprinkle with the
remaining sherry.

Lay a sheet of greaseproof paper
on top and press the cake down
well, then compress with heavy
weights. Leave to stand overnight,
then turn out on to a board.

Sprinkle a surface with icing sugar
and roll out the marzipan into a
rectangle that will completely cover
the cake. Brush the cake with the
remaining jam and press on the
marzipan. Trim if necessary.

Melt the chocolate and butter in a
heatproof bowl set over a saucepan
of hot water. Beat until smooth and
spread over the surface of the cake.
Leave until set.

If liked, dust the top with icing
sugar and serve cut into slices.

Serves 4

Celebration Shortbread

125 g (4 oz) plain flour

50 g (2 oz) rice flour

125 g (4 oz) butter

50 g (2 oz) caster sugar

50 g (2 oz) mixed chopped glacé
fruits, washed and dried, e.g.
cherries, angelica, pineapple

Topping:

40 g (1½ oz) butter

1½ tablespoons sugar

2 tablespoons milk

175 g (6 oz) icing sugar, sifted

2 tablespoons cocoa powder, sifted

Grease and base-line an 18 cm (7 inch) square sandwich tin. Sift the flours into a bowl and rub in the butter until the mixture resembles coarse breadcrumbs. Add the caster sugar and glacé fruits, then knead to a smooth dough.

Lightly press the dough into the tin. Smooth over until level and prick with a fork.

Bake in a preheated oven, 140°C (275°F), Gas Mark 1, for ¼–½ hours until the shortbread is pale golden brown. Stand for 10 minutes then carefully turn out, peel off the paper and cool on a wire rack.

When cold, return the shortbread to the sandwich tin.

To make the topping, melt the butter and sugar in the milk over a gentle heat, bring to the boil, then pour over the icing sugar and cocoa powder in a bowl. Beat until cool and stiff, then spread over the shortbread. Roughen the surface with a fork. When the topping has set, cut into bars.

Makes about 10 bars

left: Russian cake, celebration shortbread, mazariner

Mazariner

2 x quantity Chocolate Cream Pie pastry (see page 20)

50 g (2 oz) butter

50 g (2 oz) caster sugar

1 egg

50 g (2 oz) ground almonds

few drops almond essence

green food colouring

75–125 g (3–4 oz) plain chocolate, melted

about 12 blanched almonds, toasted

Roll out the pastry to about 5 mm (¼ inch) thick and use to line 12 deep tartlet or patty tins. Prick the bases with a fork.

Cream the butter and sugar until light and fluffy, then beat in the egg. Carefully fold in the ground almonds, almond essence to taste and a few drops of green food colouring to make it pale green.

Two-thirds fill each pastry case with the mixture, then bake in a preheated oven, 180°C (350°F), Gas Mark 4, for about 15 minutes until the filling is well risen. Cool on a wire rack.

Dip the top of each tart into the chocolate. Place an almond on each and cool until set.

Makes about 12

Chocolate Muesli Slice

125 g (4 oz) clear honey

125 g (4 oz) butter or block margarine

50–75 g (2–3 oz) soft brown sugar, to taste

250 g (8 oz) unsweetened muesli base

50 g (2 oz) sultanas

50 g (2 oz) hazelnuts, chopped

Topping: (optional)

125 g (4 oz) plain chocolate, chopped

25 g (1 oz) butter

1 tablespoon milk

Grease and base-line a 20 cm (8 inch) square sandwich tin. Melt the honey, butter or margarine and sugar in a saucepan. Stir in the muesli base, sultanas and hazelnuts. Mix well.

Press the mixture into the tin and spread evenly. Bake in a preheated oven, 180°C (350°F), Gas Mark 4, for 25–30 minutes until beginning to colour evenly. Remove from the oven and leave in the tin. Cool slightly.

To make the topping, if using, melt the chocolate with the butter and milk in a small heatproof bowl set over a pan of hot water. Stir until smooth. Pour over the muesli base and cool until almost set. Cut into 16 pieces and leave in the tin until cold.

Makes 16

Index